Where Research Begins

· ·

CHOOSING
A RESEARCH
PROJECT THAT
MATTERS TO
YOU (AND THE
WORLD)

Where Research Begins

· ·

Thomas S. Mullaney & Christopher Rea

The

University of

Chicago Press

Chicago and

London

The University of Chicago Press, Chicago 60637
The University of Chicago Press, Ltd., London
© 2022 by Thomas S. Mullaney and Christopher Rea
All rights reserved. No part of this book may be used or
reproduced in any manner whatsoever without written permission,
except in the case of brief quotations in critical articles and
reviews. For more information, contact the University of
Chicago Press, 1427 E. 60th St., Chicago, IL 60637.
Published 2022
Printed in the United States of America

32 31 30 29 28 27 26 25 24   4 5 6

ISBN-13: 978-0-226-80111-7 (cloth)
ISBN-13: 978-0-226-81744-6 (paper)
ISBN-13: 978-0-226-81735-4 (e-book)
DOI: https://doi.org/10.7208/chicago/9780226817354.001.0001

Library of Congress Cataloging-in-Publication Data

Names: Mullaney, Thomas S. (Thomas Shawn), author. |
    Rea, Christopher G., author.
Title: Where research begins : choosing a research project that matters to
    you (and the world) / Thomas S. Mullaney and Christopher Rea.
Other titles: Chicago guides to writing, editing, and publishing.
Description: Chicago ; London : The University of Chicago Press, 2022. |
    Series: Chicago guides to writing, editing, and publishing | Includes index.
Identifiers: LCCN 2021032879 | ISBN 9780226801117 (cloth) |
    ISBN 9780226817446 (paperback) | ISBN 9780226817354 (ebook)
Subjects: LCSH: Research.
Classification: LCC AZ105 .M85 2022 | DDC 001.4 — dc23
LC record available at https://lccn.loc.gov/2021032879

♾ This paper meets the requirements of ANSI/NISO Z39.48-1992
(Permanence of Paper).

Contents

· · · · · · · · · · · ·

Introduction

· · · · · · · · · · · · · · · · ·

In the early 2000s, when we were both in graduate school, we were assigned to teach a course on research methodology. The course was required for undergraduate majors in our department. On paper, it was taught by a professor, but in truth, everything was left to us. We had to design the course from scratch, with little guidance on how to do so. The one and only requirement was that each student had to produce a research proposal by the end of the term — a detailed plan of attack that outlined the specific questions the project sought to explore and answer, the sources they would use, and the potential implications and impact of their findings.

The two of us teamed up to map out a semester-long plan through which a student could develop a full-fledged research project in a relatively short span of time. We reflected on our own experiences, both as undergraduates and now as early-career scholars, and synthesized everything into a road map as clear as a twelve-step smoking cessation program. It covered everything, we thought: working with primary sources, taking notes, compiling an annotated bibliography of secondary sources, developing a hypothesis, outlining the structure of a thesis, and summarizing the expected implications of the study.

By following our plan, each student's paper would come together piece by piece.

Or so we thought.

Something went wrong. As soon as the class started, our

plan unraveled. Each week, the two of us met to compare notes, and we noticed a disturbing pattern: despite our "easy-to-follow road map," our students were stuck, struggling just to get out of the garage, let alone make the cross-country journey we had charted out. *How do I build a bibliography when I don't know what I want to work on? I have general interests, but no questions — how do I ask the right questions? How can my questions have "implications" when I don't even know what my questions are? I read a source and found it interesting — but how should I come up with a thesis?*

Half the semester raced by, and most students had yet to settle on a project idea that excited them. Everyone fell terribly behind. Without a research question, how could they "delve into sources" or "form a hypothesis?" How could they possibly transform their passion into a project if they weren't sure what their passion was?

Some students chose to settle, selecting a topic that they didn't feel any particular passion for, and then dutifully working through our program. But it was plain to see that they had chosen their topics simply because *they had to choose something.* As the deadline approached, anxiety mounted for the students and for us.

The mistake we made is easy to see in hindsight: we forgot that the most challenging part of research is the part *before you begin,* when you don't know what questions you want to ask or what problem you want to solve. The research process doesn't begin *after* you figure out your core questions. The research process begins *before* you know what you are researching. This is the fundamental irony of research, an irony that no research guide teaches you how to navigate.

This book is the result of our combined experience — decades of teaching, along with years of reflecting on the discovery we made as we struggled and failed to help a group of highly skilled and motivated students begin their research journeys. What we discovered is this: there are many books out there that explain the "research process" to researchers who *already know what their question or problem is*, but not one that helps a student figure out what their question or problem is in the first place. Those books do a masterful job of explaining how to outline, draft, revise, cite sources, and more. And they do an effective job of instructing young researchers how to choose the appropriate scale for their research projects. They may keep you on track if you already know your direction. But none of them teach you what to do *before* you know where you're going. None of them teach you *where to begin*.

Why are there so many books on how to do research, yet so few on how to figure out *what* you are trying to research? This is not hard to explain. The assumption is that the average person already knows what their "passion" is, and just needs to follow it. A passion, we imagine, is something that everyone already has, and is fully aware of.

We have a different take on things. While we do believe that all people have passions, we do *not* assume that everyone already knows what theirs are. We can have passions we are unable to articulate in words. We can even have passions we are *entirely unaware we have*—either because we don't know ourselves all that well, or because we never realized that our particular set of curiosities and concerns "counted" as a passion. Even more confusingly, we sometimes guess incorrectly about where our true passions lie. This happens far more often than we might think. After all, we all live our lives surrounded by external expectations (social, cultural, familial, real, imagined), and it's hard not to adopt some or all of these expectations as our own. Rather than learning the craft of introspection or self-trust, we opt for a quicker route: we take on the passions that *other* people have, and pretend as best we can that these passions are ours.

In other words, when faced with the question of *where* to begin our research, we too often look outside ourselves. We seek external validation. We let others set our agenda. But research begins with the researcher identifying the problem they carry *inside* them and figuring out what to do with it. This is what we failed to recognize back when we taught our very first class. Without meaning to, we shortchanged our students. With more time for introspection, they'd have had a far more rewarding research experience.

We have reunited nearly twenty years later to make things right. This book is the course we wish we had taught decades ago. We call the guiding principle underpinning this book *Self-Centered Research*.

Self-Centered Research: A Manifesto

In this book, we advocate a "self-centered" approach to research. Focusing on the early stages of the research process, we empower you with a variety of techniques and a mindset that will help you begin your research journey in the right direction — pointed toward a problem that matters deeply to *you*.

What is Self-Centered Research, and why do it?

Let's begin by clarifying what the term means — and what it doesn't.

Self-Centered Research is the following:

1. A *practice* of research that emphasizes the importance of setting out on the research journey from exactly where you are *right now*, and maintaining close contact with your own self — your instincts, your curiosities, and your biases — throughout the process. To be a "self-centered" researcher is to maintain your center of gravity over your own two feet at all times, and to avoid pursuing topics and questions that you imagine might please some imaginary, external judge.
2. An *ethic* of research that involves consciously acknowledging and assessing your abilities and your limitations as a researcher. It involves being *centered*: knowing who you are, listening to your own

instincts, trusting them even when they sound naive or inarticulate, and refining them during the research process.

3. A *state of mind* that affirms the value of your ideas, assumptions, and concerns in shaping your agenda and the direction of your research. It presumes that the better (and faster) you figure out your own concerns and motivations as a researcher, the better (and faster) you will discover a research problem that is deeply meaningful both to you *and* to the world at large. But the first person who must be deeply concerned with your research problem is *you, the researcher*.

Now that we've said what Self-Centered Research is, let's be clear about what it *isn't*.

Self-Centered Research does *not* mean unleashing (or inflating) your ego. Being self-*centered* is not being self-absorbed, self-obsessed, self-congratulatory, self-consumed, self-indulgent, self-involved, self-serving, or self-ish.

Quite the opposite: self-centered researchers are self-reflexive, and always self-critical; honest and probing about their own interests, motivations, and abilities; but also open and confident enough to assess the validity of others'. This means having the wherewithal to challenge received wisdom, including unfounded ideas you are probably carrying around without realizing it.

Self-Centered Research is also not autobiographical. It does not imply that the papers, articles, reports, or books you write will tell the story of your life. Or that every documentary you produce, or painting you paint, will be a self-portrait.

The end goal of the Self-Centered Research process is, just like conventional research processes, one in which the researcher produces empirical, grounded, theoretically informed, and compelling scholarship about some aspect of the world around us, and does so in a way that changes how *other* people think. In order to identify and solve a problem that truly matters to other people, however, the Self-Centered Research process insists that this problem must matter, first and foremost, to *you*.

The first precondition of excellent scholarship, in other words, is that the focus of your research must be more than just a passing interest, a "good idea," or something that was assigned to you by an outside party.

We'll take you through a process of generating questions — questions that are of concern to you — and show how, through your passion and your labor, they can become questions that are of concern to others.

Centered Research Is the Best Research

One of the things that makes research so fantastic is also what makes it so daunting: you could, theoretically, research *anything*.

Where to begin?

The answer is: Exactly where you are, right now.

Core to this book are two propositions. First, research can be a life-changing experience, if you get a few things right from the start. Second, the most important part of beginning a research project is finding your center. Research is a process not just of solving problems but of finding problems that you — and other people — didn't know existed. It's a process of discovery, analysis, and creation that can generate its own momentum and create a virtuous cycle of inspiration. Deep-seated problems only reveal themselves through self-trust, exposure to primary sources, and time. Only you — not anyone else — can tell you what you were meant to research. Answering the question "What to research?" requires a hard look in the mirror.

So if you are the only person who can answer the question "What to research?" why read this book?

A fair question.

We do not pretend to have a secret formula for generating research projects. We cannot tell you *what* to research. What we can offer are specific techniques designed to accelerate a generative process that will have you asking questions that lead you to discover your underlying research problem, and then make an actual project out of it.

The goal of this book, then, is to help you create the ideal conditions to start a fire in your mind—a "fire that lights itself," to borrow a phrase that jazz drummer Buddy Rich used to describe genius. But at the same time, it will show you how to maintain balance and clarity in situations of complexity, uncertainty, and ambiguity. And it will teach you ways to tell the difference between *unproductive* uncertainty—that is, when you're on the wrong path, and should probably turn back—and *productive* uncertainty—that is, when it may *feel* like you're lost, but where your inner instinct and wisdom are encouraging you to keep on going.

If you're casting about for your first research topic, we'll help you get started. If you have lots of good ideas and need no help in generating questions, we'll help you figure out which ideas and questions to invest your time in. If you already have a well-defined project, we'll teach you how to deepen and refine your research, uncovering possibilities you didn't know existed. If you are a veteran researcher or teacher, you will find in this book a philosophy of research and a repertoire of strategies you can share with students and even use to refine your own practice.

This book is designed to be practical, first and foremost, providing specific and tested techniques to help you

- choose a research topic;
- transform this topic into a set of concrete and compelling questions;
- identify the underlying problem motivating the questions you're asking;

- deal with the assumptions, biases, and preconceived notions you might have about your topic;
- articulate the stakes involved in this problem and prioritize competing interests and concerns;
- approach and navigate the broader community of researchers who work on the same "topic" as you (that is, your "major" or "field");
- discover and map out relevant researcher communities that exist beyond your field;
- find sources that will be useful to your research project;
- use the sources you find to refine your questions further (especially during the preliminary research stage);
- deal with mental roadblocks and keep up your momentum during the critical early stages of your project, when it's easiest to feel lost;
- remain flexible, nimble, astute, and motivated as a researcher.

This set of skills is in short supply everywhere. While we use the language of the academy — talking about papers, theses, students, classes, and teachers — these skills are fundamental to a variety of fields and professions. The ideas and exercises you'll read about here have applications in business, journalism, art, design, engineering, community-building, and entrepreneurship. The skills described in this book are fundamental to research, meaning that they will help you no matter your field of inquiry or level of research expertise.

How to Use This Book

Here are the keys to using this book, no matter what your research background:

- **Write as you go.** This is our #1 recommendation, as the most important work you'll be doing is documenting your interests, assumptions, problems, and ideas — what we will refer to as "self-evidence." The process we outline in this book is not meant to be carried out in your head, and you will need a written record of your thoughts for many of the exercises. Write in whatever form suits you: pad and pen, digital, back of napkin, whiteboard, or slate. You'll be coming back to this self-evidence again and again. Err on the side of writing too much. (We say more about why to write so much in the first exercise below.)

- **Repeat exercises, readings, and writing as needed.** *Everything* in this book is designed to be done more than once, especially when you . . .
- **Apply the exercises to your own project** (but if you don't have a project yet, don't worry!). We have some examples prepared, but you will achieve your goals only when you apply the ideas presented here to your own work.

Interspersed throughout the book you will find three recurring sections, which offer ways of putting ideas into practice at different stages of the research-inception process:

- Try This Now
- Commonly Made Mistakes
- Sounding Board

TRY THIS NOW

In each chapter, you will work through practical exercises and games designed to help you achieve a specific set of goals: generating questions, refining questions, discovering the patterns that connect your questions, and identifying the problem that motivates you. We believe that different approaches are effective for different researchers, so we offer a variety of exercises. All of the exercises rely on a core set of principles. These include

- attentive, nonjudgmental self-observation;
- giving oneself permission and encouragement to say inarticulate, tentative, and vulnerable things out loud;
- getting things down on paper.

We encourage you to read this book from start to finish, but you might also choose to jump around. Research is a recursive and iterative process, not a linear one. Likewise, this book is designed to be reread. Whether or not you tackle everything in sequence on your first pass, the only way to get the benefit of our advice is by completing the exercises, and, as mentioned above, by *writing things down.*

The point of all this continual writing is to produce what we term "evidence of self," or "self-evidence." You can think of self-evidence as clues that will help you figure out the answers to the most important questions that a researcher must answer during this early phase: *Why am I concerned with this topic? What is it about this subject that I think holds the key to some larger issue? Why does this primary source jump out at me? Why, out of all possible topics that I could be working on, do I keep coming back to this one? What is my Problem?*

Self-evidence is a valuable form of note-taking that we believe many researchers neglect. Perhaps they dismiss it as a form of "me-search" diary-keeping. Subjective, anecdotal information, the thinking goes, might be useful should someone ever produce a "making-of" documentary about your project, but it is not *real* research. We disagree, and we suspect that researchers who harbor such prejudice could benefit from more introspection.

We advocate making introspection a habitual part of your research method. The pieces of self-evidence you produce during the Self-Centered Research process are cousins to the kind of notes experienced researchers routinely make when they read primary sources, conduct interviews, carry out ethnographic fieldwork, or copy down bibliographic information. We call them *self*-evidence because, during this early phase of research, these notes will possess a value that goes far beyond the recording of facts, quotes, observations, and other evidence about the world around you. They will provide evidence about *you yourself*. With these clues you will be able to uncover the hidden questions and problems you carry around inside you. Discover them early in the research process and not only will you save yourself time and frustration, but, more importantly, you will be more likely to arrive at the research project that is right for you.

COMMONLY MADE MISTAKES

A list of these follows each "Try This Now" exercise. Most of these mistakes fall into one of three categories:

1. Not letting yourself be vulnerable
2. Not listening to yourself
3. Not writing things down

In guiding other researchers and students through these exercises, we've seen how hard it can be to avoid the impulses to protect yourself (that is, to be defensive), and to listen to the voices of imagined authorities, which promote certain lines of inquiry and inhibit others.

These bad habits set up inadvertent roadblocks to introspection. Knowing about commonly made mistakes, we are better equipped to avoid those impulses and to focus on nonjudgmental self-observation. Writing things down during the process is essential because those written records will become the basis for the self-observation that will help your project come together. Don't try to remember everything. Insight can be fleeting. And, as we'll remind you again and again, don't wait till the very end. Write your thoughts down now.

SOUNDING BOARD

From time to time, you might find it useful to bounce your ideas off a Sounding Board — a teacher, mentor, friend, colleague, or other adviser. We suggest specific ways to prepare for such conversations. A Sounding Board is someone who helps you to gain alternative perspectives on your ideas and writings and to step outside yourself. They help you to become aware of aspects of your ideas that didn't occur to you at first, or perhaps identify unconscious tendencies in your thinking. A Sounding Board helps you to self-reflect and make better decisions, so we recommend that you make talking to someone you trust a habit early in the research process. Ultimately, the Self-Centered Research process will empower you to become your own Sounding Board.

Every Sounding Board moment comes with an important caveat. Well-meaning suggestions from a teacher, adviser, or other authority figure — suggestions as to what you "could" or "should" work on — can have a major impact on a researcher during the early phases of research. If you feel lost, or uncertain about the value of your nascent ideas, a suggestion from a boss, teacher, or adviser (especially an overbearing one) can feel a lot like a *command.* Or it may become your fallback, your "Well, I can't come up with anything better, so I might as well go with that!" A friendly lead might seem like a way to speed things up. What if you skipped all that messy introspection and snapped up the ready-made idea that your trusted adviser has told you is important? Unfortunately, the effect can be inhibitory and counterproductive.

As mentors ourselves, we have seen many students latch onto the first idea we floated by them and, months later, produce a paper that left us unconvinced was one *they* were really interested in writing. The result is typically suboptimal. The point of research is not to fall back, it's to move forward — to take a risk and discover or create something original. A mentor can offer advice that saves you from retracing others' paths to the same conclusion. But when a student comes with an idea for a research project and asks, "Is this what you want?" a true mentor's response is always the same: "Is this what *you* want?"

In our experience, if a research question is *not* one that you're truly motivated to spend your time answering, you'll find it a challenge to do a good job, or even to finish. So, even before you meet with your Sounding Board and even before getting too deeply into research sources, follow the steps in the first part of this book to find your center.

Introversion, First. Extroversion, Second.

The two-part process of starting a research project involves looking first inward and then outward. Part 1 takes you through the inward-focused process of becoming a self-centered researcher. You will reflect on the experiences, interests, priorities, and assumptions you bring with you — and assess how to make best use of them in charting out a research direction. This process goes beyond conventional brainstorming because it requires taking stock of your values. It involves distinguishing between what *doesn't* matter to you, what you *think* matters to you, and what *really* matters to you.

We believe that you are best off starting this process *before* you field-test your ideas against the wisdom of the research community. Ideas abound — not all of equal merit — and even at this early stage in your research you'll want to be judicious in evaluating which of them should influence your project. Authorities also abound (again, not all of equal merit), and they can exert undue influence on the direction of research at this vulnerable stage when you're not quite sure yet just what you want to do.

Having taken those steps toward becoming a self-centered researcher, you'll then be ready to test and refine your project ideas in relation to the questions, methodologies, theories, protocols, assumptions, and collective experiences of the research community. Part 2 focuses on this process of *extroversion*. It helps you to navigate the often bewildering process of coming to terms with the research communities conventionally known as "fields" and "disciplines," as well as how to identify researchers who may not be in the same field as you but who are interested in similar problems — what we call your Problem Collective. Fields and disciplines tend to be easy to identify by their departments, associations, journals, and degrees. A Problem Collective is less self-evident, and as it is a key concept of this book, it comes first in Part 2.

TRY THIS NOW: Write Here, Right Now
The goal: *To make writing a habitual part of the research idea-generation process. You can start by creating a record of your research thoughts, speculations, and goals even before you have a fully formed project.*

Now it's time to start writing. That's right—here, now, on this page.

As mentioned above, this is a *workbook*. It is not a pep talk before the big game. It is not a prelude to action. Nor is it a lecture to be taken in passively. We have written part of this book, but you will be writing *the most important part of the book* as you go along. Treat this book as a guide, a reference manual, and a coloring book. Fill up the margins with questions, ideas, and doubts. Underline, highlight, dog-ear.

Every section of this book—including this introduction— contains writing activities and exercises designed to help you start writing *even as you think through your research goals, priorities, and plans*. As we'll reemphasize throughout the book, research is not a linear process, and therefore the writing you do now is not a form of "prewriting" that generates verbiage to be later thrown away. It is not a warm-up. The writing you do now is *part of the core research process*, which involves generating ideas, recording them, reflecting on them, refining them based on new information, and continually searching for better ways to ask and articulate them.

All of the writing you do with (and in) this book will help the research process by

- creating an evolving record of your ideas—your "self-evidence";
- continually externalizing your thoughts, as an aid to memory and to your research collaborators;
- building your project step-by-step through different types of writing, focused on discrete aspects of the early phases of research;
- making writing a regular research habit.

So, in the space below, express what you currently think you want to accomplish with your research project. What topics or questions interest you? What would "success" be for you? What is your ideal research outcome? And remember: no pressure. You're writing for no one but yourself.

COMMONLY MADE MISTAKES
- Writing for someone else. There is no need to impress, to sound important, or to rationalize your goals in this brainstorm. Just write what you think you want to research.

Part 1

· · · · · · · · · · · ·

Become a Self-Centered Researcher

Part 1 of this book guides you through the process of centering your research questions, of aligning them with the concerns that you carry inside you. These are questions and concerns about life, about the world, even about existence itself. This doesn't mean that your research will be ethereal and philosophical, or autobiographical. You will not be writing *about* yourself, but rather *from* yourself, instead of from external sources. This is a process of self-reflective decision-making that is crucial at the inception stage of a research project.

The goal of this stage is to make sure that you are fully aware of your own motivations and values, are confident of your priorities, and have taken stock of your assets, capabilities, and limitations. Go through these steps, and you'll emerge with the self-assurance and self-possession a researcher needs to be able to make the most of the multiple voices and agendas out there in the broader research community—a process we detail in part 2.

The basic process goes like this. In chapter 1, we teach you how to transform a vague and grand-sounding topic (whether you came up with it yourself, or someone assigned it to you) into a set of concrete, down-to-earth, yet still preliminary questions. In chapter 2, you will learn how to analyze the questions you created in chapter 1, discovering the patterns that connect some, most, or perhaps all of them. Suddenly, what at first may have appeared to be a random set of questions will start to add up to form a coherent picture. This is the second major milestone you will reach: the identification of your Research Problem, capital *R*, capital *P*. In chapter 3, you will learn to take your questions, and your Problem, and turn them into a viable research project rooted in primary sources.

Above all, part 1 shows why a shift in thinking — from relying on polished, externally oriented language to justify one's instinctual curiosities, to relying on internal, modest, and often inarticulate language — is so important in the early stages of research. Part 1 teaches you how to avoid the ever-present risk of outsmarting yourself.

1. Questions

. . . .

This chapter helps you navigate the first challenge you will face in your research process: How do you transform broad and vague "topics" of interest into a set of concrete and (for you, at least) fascinating *questions*? In the earliest phases of research, most people don't have specific questions in mind. They have *topics of interest.* You have already started recording some of your own in the introduction. The main challenge is not identifying potential topics of interest, but in moving from these generic topics to a specific set of questions. While seemingly straightforward, this surprisingly demanding process requires a mix of confidence and vulnerability.

A Topic Is Not a Question

Topics are wonderful things to have. They're useful at the beginning of any research project. A topic suggests a field or scope of inquiry. It empowers. It gives a sense of identity and purpose. I work on . . . the Harlem Renaissance, Soviet history, women's studies, experimental poetry, urban planning, environmental history. Having a topic makes one feel solid, self-aware, oriented.

Topics can be deceptive, however. They are immense and abstract categories. They organize universities, businesses, and research organizations — the Department of Topic X, the Institute for Topic Y. They show up on business cards: Professor of Topic Q. They shape how we think about the world.

But their use to the researcher is limited for one very obvious reason: a topic is not a question.

How do topics and questions differ? Let us count the ways (see table 1).

TABLE 1. DISTINGUISH BETWEEN A TOPIC AND A QUESTION

A TOPIC	A QUESTION
Is a noun, perhaps with a modifier	Is a sentence with a question mark at the end
May be broad or specific	May be broad or specific
Indicates an area of curiosity	Indicates an area of curiosity, and some sense of how you will satisfy that curiosity
Raises innumerable questions, but often ones that pull in a thousand different directions	Raises more specific, related questions
Has no answer	Has an answer—and sometimes several

You can see already how topics can even be *obstacles* to the research process. When a researcher tells you what topic they're interested in, more often than not they leave you wondering which of the many possible pathways and potential questions about that topic they intend to follow, or why the topic matters to them. Simply put, when we speak about topics, we could be speaking about *anything* (and thus *nothing*) at all.

Harlem Renaissance *what*? Soviet economic history *how*? Environmental history *where*? When someone tells you what their topic is, you actually still know very little about what drives them as a researcher, much less what direction their research takes. A study of the Harlem Renaissance might turn out to be about urban migration. But it could just as readily be about poetry, intellectual history, or housing markets. A researcher working on Soviet economic history might be interested in the history of steel production technology, labor relations during World War II, or perhaps the development of economic think tanks in Moscow. Likewise, research on environmental history might be interested in invasive species, hydroelectric dams, or fire-stick farming. There's simply no way to know. All of these avenues (and many more) are equally probable, yet some might be of *no interest* to the researcher — some of these potential avenues might even bore them to tears. A person working on environmental history might have more in common with a scholar of the Harlem Renaissance than with their "fellow" environmental historians. By themselves, topics are not very good guides for the research process. That's why they can be dangerous.

When you have a topic and are struggling to turn it into a project, the common advice you will hear is "Narrow it down."

We call this the *Narrow-Down-Your-Topic Trap.*

Its seemingly straightforward logic — a "narrow" topic is easier to work on than a "broad" topic — leads many researchers, especially inexperienced ones, into dead ends. A more discrete scope that reduces the volume of sources you need to analyze can, to be sure, answer the *when* and *where* questions. But a topic alone — even a "narrow" one — is insufficient, because it still leaves unanswered the *how* and *why* questions. Tell someone your "narrow" topic, and they may still have no clue what you're doing. Even a "narrow" topic cannot tell *you* what to do.

Simply put, *you cannot "narrow" your way out of Topic Land.*

Every researcher needs to figure out *what to do* and *how to do it*. And — assuming that you want to devote your time and energy to something worthwhile — the question that comes before *what* and *how* is *why*.

A brief example: a student sat down with Tom to discuss

potential paper topics for a history course. The topic of the paper, the student explained, would be Chinese geomancy, or feng shui. In feng shui, the landscape and the natural environment are understood to be energetically alive, with this energy having the capacity to affect — for better or for worse — the fortunes of the living, as well as the afterlives of the deceased. By building one's home or city in harmony with the logics and flows of these energetic forces, one can improve one's fortune. Neglecting or violating these logics can bring ruin.

Feng shui is a promising and potentially fascinating topic, to be sure, but Tom was still unclear about the student's concerns. What were the student's *questions* about the topic? What was at stake for them? *Why feng shui?*

The student was equipped with a "straight-A" vocabulary, and had clearly rehearsed prior to the meeting, using key terms and concepts from the course. Feng shui offered a way to examine "Chinese modernity," the student explained, to examine "knowledge production" during China's transition from "tradition" to "modernity." Everything about the presentation was polished.

Something was still missing, though.

OK, but why feng shui? *If the main motivation is to understand "Chinese modernity," your paper doesn't need to be on* feng shui. *You could just as easily have chosen to work on education reform, the development of chemistry, or perhaps the history of translation. There are an infinite number of ways to "get at" the issue of modernity.*

The student tried again, pulling out all the stops by using as many "smart-sounding" justifications as possible. There were "gaps in the literature," they explained, using an academic code word to mean "important areas in our map of knowledge that have yet to be filled in." Feng shui had the makings of a powerful "intervention" in the historiography, they suggested, using another word commonly heard in the academy. In other words, the student was trying to speak in code with Tom, using terminology they assumed would resonate with an academic mentor.

It all still begged the question. To say that there is a "gap in the literature" is to assume that the topic in question is of unquestionable importance and needs to be addressed. *But important to whom, and why?* Besides, "gaps" in human knowledge are infinite. Why fill *this* particular gap?

The impasse cannot simply be blamed on the student being "inexperienced." Most researchers (even seasoned ones) instinctually try to justify their incipient research ideas using the vocabulary of "importance" or "significance"— as defined by an imaginary, *external* judge. But at the outset, external judges are not what we need. Instead, what every researcher needs in the earliest phase of a project is to answer a question that is profoundly personal: Out of the infinite number of potential topics of interest, why am I drawn to *this* one? If I had to guess, what is my connection with *this* topic? Why is it so magnetic to me?

There was a noticeable pause in the conversation, and the student's entire disposition shifted. The tone and volume of the voice softened. Even the posture relaxed. Suddenly, the conversation felt less like a performance, in which the student was trying to impress the professor. Instead, the exchange became more open, even vulnerable. The student allowed themself to share more fundamental concerns, to stop acting intelligent and just *be* intelligent.

My mom is a lawyer, the student continued. *She's highly educated and is the most rational person I know. She's not superstitious at all. But she also believes in* feng shui *— truly believes in it — and I just can't understand how.*

All of a sudden, the room was full of new questions. *What else might a "rational" person not believe in, do you think? Meditation? Yoga? Reflexology? Numerology? What about psychiatry, or perhaps economics? Who or what defines this "rational/irrational" boundary? Is this boundary the same in all parts of the world? How and when have views about rationality taken shape in history? Why? What might I find if I looked at primary sources from other time periods, or other cultures? What do I mean by "rational" anyway? Why am I using that word? Is it because "rationality" depends on logic, and I think* feng shui *is illogical? Or is there another reason I think* feng shui *and rationality are incompatible?*

It was like getting away from the glare of the city lights — suddenly, the sky was filled with stars.

The questions went on, filling the student's notepad.

A few key aspects of the discussion led to this break-through. Here's how we'd phrase them for a researcher trying to move from a topic to questions:

1. **Make yourself vulnerable.** The student sounded unpolished (as they had initially worried) — *but that's a good thing.* The questions one generates during this early phase are not final products. Many things in our lives coach us against opening up. We want to appear mature and professional, and we hesitate to ask questions that might make us appear unpolished or naive. But at this stage, our questions don't need to be polished or even coherent. All they have to be is *honest, to the best of our knowledge.* Trust yourself.

2. **Keep the conversation affirmative and nonjudgmental.** Neither the researcher nor the Sounding Board said anything to denigrate the researcher's assumptions about rationality. At the brainstorming stage, it's easy to shut down lines of inquiry prematurely, with inhibitory thoughts or statements like *Your assumptions are wrong: there is nothing inherently irrational about non-Western practices!* Or perhaps by chiding oneself with high-level language like *My concept of rationality is clearly a "social construction."* Resist the temptation. Far better is simply to allow the questions to proliferate, no matter how seemingly unimportant, naive,

incoherent, scattered, or biased they might seem. Whether you're working alone or with someone else, the goal at this point is simply to generate questions. We'll discuss how to use them later on.

3. **Write down your ideas.** The researcher and Sounding Board wrote down all the questions as they spilled out. Ideas can come rapidly, but they can be forgotten rapidly too if not recorded. As we will emphasize again and again, during this early phase of research, thinking about things is not enough. You need to get things down in writing, to create traces of thought that you can later use for other purposes.

4. **Generate questions internally.** In the conversation described above, it was the student who was producing questions; the Sounding Board barely needed to chime in. The questions you should be aiming at now are those driven by your own knowledge, assumptions, and curiosities. At this point, don't try to think from the "outside in" by trying to generate questions you think might satisfy some imaginary judge.

This particular student was in a more fortunate position than most, having clearly done a great deal of self-reflection in advance of the meeting. They were already aware of why their topic mattered to them personally and simply had to overcome reluctance to share those reasons.

For most of us, the challenge is greater. We might be drawn to a particular topic without having any idea why. Or, perhaps more accurately, *some part of us knows why*, but the *rest* of us — the part of us that has to field questions like "Why does that interest you?"— still has absolutely no idea.

As we progress through the stages of Self-Centered Research, we'll discuss several ways to close the distance between these two parts of ourselves. You will learn how to bring together

- the *intuitive* part of you that knows, but cannot speak;
- the *executive* part of you that speaks, but does not know.

Questions lead us in specific directions—whether toward specific answers or to primary sources that we need to answer the questions or to the work of fellow scholars who are grappling with similar questions (i.e., secondary sources) or, more often than not, to more and better questions. Questions force a self-reckoning.

Questions have another virtue. Every question a person asks about the world is a piece of "self-evidence" about the researcher—evidence that helps the researcher reflect on their own intellectual, emotional, and personal motivations for asking the question in the first place. The goal here is to explain, rather than simply assert, one's interest in a topic.

Consider the following example:

Soviet history is fascinating.

Questions give much more self-evidence:

Given the Soviet Union's vociferous critique of capitalism, did it develop its own form of accounting practices? The USSR must have had accountants to keep track of economic data, and yet most accounting theory to that point had been developed in capitalist contexts — was that a problem for the Soviets?

Now you have more clues to answer the obvious question, *Why are you interested in that?* Your questions place you in the hot seat. They require you to ask probing questions about yourself, without falling back on vague and tautological responses like "The topic is interesting, which is why I'm interested in it!"

TRY THIS NOW: Search Yourself

The goal: *To use a list of primary-source search results to figure out the aspects of your topic that most interest you, and draft questions based on these interests.*

You already know how to search the internet. This exercise prompts you to use the results of an internet search to *search yourself*.

This exercise offers one way to get from a topic to questions.

Here's a quick summary of the steps of this exercise, before we dive into details about each:

1. Based on the "Try This Now" exercise you completed in the introduction, write down any and all of the research topics you are drawn to. Feel free to be as general as possible, and to include more than one.

2. Select one of the topics on your list and run a search using at least three (or more) of the web-based databases listed below. (You can find more on whereresearchbegins.com.)

3. Click on a few of the search results that interest you—say, five to ten.

4. Don't read the search results in depth. Instead, your goal is to dedicate (a) perhaps 20 percent of your mental energy to scanning the list of search results (and perhaps the contents of a few) and (b) the remaining 80 percent of your mental energy to self-observation. You want to read yourself as you read the results.

5. In particular, pay close attention to how your mind and body are responding to different search results: Which ones seem to jump out at you? Which ones cause you to linger just a split second longer? Which ones quicken your pulse, even slightly?

6. Write down at least ten entries that attract you, without worrying about why they do.
7. Based on this list of ten entries, answer the three questions on page 31 about those entries, to generate self-evidence.
8. Sleep on it (take a break of at least twenty-four hours).
9. Return to the answers you wrote out and ask yourself: If I didn't know the person who wrote these answers, or flagged these search results as "interesting," what kinds of guesses would I make about this researcher? What story does this "self-evidence" seem to tell about the researcher, in terms of their concerns and interests?
10. Write down your thoughts on these questions, getting as much down on paper as possible.

Let's dive in a bit deeper.

Step 1 is straightforward enough.

Step 2: Select a database. We list a few good choices here, and you can find dozens more at whereresearch begins.com.

- WorldCat: www.worldcat.org
- HathiTrust: https://www.hathitrust.org
- Trove: https://trove.nla.gov.au
- Online Archive of California (OAC): www.oac.cdlib .org
- Archives Portal Europe: http://www.archivesportal europe.net
- Collaborative European Digital Archive Infrastructure (CENDARI): www.cendari.eu
- Consortium of European Research Libraries (CERL): https://www.cerl.org/resources/main

Don't worry about choosing the "right" database for your topic. For the purposes of this exercise, it really doesn't matter which one you choose. (You'll see why in a moment.) And don't worry about where the library is located, geographically. If you imagine you're unlikely to find anything in a New Jersey–based archive about, say, Armenian politics, or anything in a Kansas-based archive on Etruscan pottery, you might be surprised.

Familiarize yourself briefly with how the search engine works, and then run a basic query. Enter your search term—your topic, or some variation thereof—and see what comes up. If your search yields zero results, try a more generic search term, or perhaps a related but different one. If all else fails, go to a different site and try again. The database itself is not the vital part.

Step 3: Once you get a set of search results—any results—your work is simple. Just scroll through and scan the results to see what you find. Click on a few and read them. On most of these sites, you won't be able to view the original source, only the catalogue entry. But even if a site does offer full text results, try not to get caught up in any one source for too long at this point. This is not yet the time for close reading.

Instead—and this is key—while scrolling through your search results, try to imagine that you are strapped to an EKG machine that is recording the electrical pulses going through your system *as you read*. Which primary sources raise your heart rate, even slightly? Write them down. Which ones have no effect on you one way or another? Take note of them too (since, a bit later on, we will also be taking stock of things that *bore* you!).

The goal right now, as we said above, is to "read your-self" as you read other things. As you read through the search results, only 20 percent of your cognitive energy should be dedicated to clicking on links, reading snippets of sources, and the like. The other 80 percent—and the critical part—should be dedicated to *paying attention to yourself as "you" pay attention to the sources.*

Why bother? How does this get a researcher any closer to discovering their research direction?

Well, consider this: every day our physical senses are so bombarded by stimuli that most sights, sounds, and smells go unnoticed. In fact, if we tried to pay attention to all of these stimuli all the time, our systems would get so overloaded that we would be incapable of carrying out even basic tasks. As a consequence, our bodies have evolved into refined filtration systems that decide what to ignore. Our bodies and minds have evolved into amazing not-seeing, not-feeling, not-smelling, not-hearing, and not-tasting machines.

Given how efficient we are at *ignoring* stimuli, it follows that when we *do* take notice of something—however small or insignificant—we should *take notice that we're noticing.* This form of self-evidence gives a potential clue about our underlying concerns and curiosities.

Put plainly, whenever your mind takes notice of something—*anything*—you can be certain that there is a question there, even if you are not sure what that question is.

Learn to pay attention to these clues, and then to uncover the questions whose presence they indicate, and you'll be able to move quickly and effectively from generic topics to precise and generative *questions.*

"Noticing what you are noticing" can be surprisingly difficult. You need to listen very closely to yourself, since the act of noticing something is rarely a dramatic affair. Epiphanies are not always loud. You might utter a semi-audible *Hmm*. Moments of *Eureka!* can even be silent. You might simply grin or furrow your brow or linger on an image or a line of text just a little bit longer than normal. No one needs help to hear a sonic boom. Your job here is more akin to detecting the faintest of gravitational waves.

Step 4: Go back to your search results. Write down, circle, or asterisk the ones that seem to have *any* effect on you, however small. Write a list out by hand, copy and paste the titles of the sources into a text file, or click a checkbox to save those sources in a folder or email. However you choose to do it, take notes.

To repeat: take note of anything that jumps out at you, even if it seems completely unrelated to your topic.

Let's say you run a search on the Ottomans or New Jersey or China, and in addition to "relevant" materials pertaining to the empire, the state, or the country, your list also includes what appear to be fluke materials about Ottoman furniture, Jersey cows, or porcelain china. Do not dismiss these out of hand. Scan them too. If any of them make you pause or wonder about something, make a note just as you would for any other item. Don't worry if your list seems incoherent or inconsistent. Your only job at this stage is to listen to yourself, and to take note of everything that attracts you. The winnowing comes later.

Step 5: Once you have an initial list of at least ten items (don't simply copy and paste *everything*, although definitely err on the side of inclusion rather than exclusion), take thirty minutes or so to ask yourself three questions about each item, setting down your answers in writing:

- What does this make me think of?
- If I had to venture a guess, why did I notice this one?
- What questions come to mind for me when I look at this search result?

A few words per item will do. And keep in mind: at this stage, it is quite likely that you won't know why each item attracted your attention. Some of your answers to these questions might end up feeling tentative or silly. That's OK. Just remember: as in the case of the feng shui example, avoid the temptation to act smart or to use language designed to impress some imaginary, external judge. Your only audience is you, so allow yourself to be inarticulate, instinctual, and honest. *Why did this jump out at me?*

Step 6: Put your list away, and don't look at it for a full day. We mean it. Close this book and your computer, and set a timer for twenty-four hours.

Step 7: Now return to your list with fresh eyes. Imagine for a moment that someone you don't know wrote it. If this list was all you had to go on, what would you say this researcher is concerned with? If you didn't know their topic, what would you guess is their primary concern? Since you do know the topic, does the list of "noticings" tell the *same* story or a *slightly different* story or an *extremely different* one? Are their concerns intrinsic to the topic? If so, *which aspect* of the topic? Or is the topic merely a *case of* or the *vehicle for* a different question? Write out your thoughts on paper.

COMMONLY MADE MISTAKES
- Not writing things down
- Getting bogged down in individual sources too soon
- Excluding "fluke" search results that seem unrelated to the keywords you entered in the database or unrelated to your topic
- Feigning interest in a search result that seems "important," even if it doesn't really interest you
- Only registering interest in search results for which

you think you know *why* you're interested in them, instead of being more inclusive

- Trying to make a list of noticings that is coherent and fits together
- When speculating about why a search result jumped out at you, worrying about whether or not the reason is "important," based on some imagined external standard

TRY THIS NOW: Let Boredom Be Your Guide

The goal: *To become attentive to your active dislikes, identifying questions that you "should" (in theory) be interested in based on your topic of interest, but aren't. By understanding what you* don't *care about regarding your topic, you accelerate the process of figuring out what you* do *care about.*

In the exercise above, you took notice of all of the search results that appealed to you. But what about the search results that had a *negative* impact—that seemed *boring* to you? Quite likely, they also registered on your imaginary EKG readout, but not because they attracted you. Rather, they *repelled* you, and so it's unlikely that you included them in your list. After all, the most common reaction human beings have to boredom is *avoidance*. We try to dismiss or ignore things that bore us.

Don't. Boredom is a powerful teacher, and deserves our attention. Boredom is not the same thing as disinterest or lack of interest. It is not a passive experience. Boredom is an *active* sentiment, a *rejection* of something that, like excitement, provides you with more self-evidence through which you can understand your concerns and motivations more clearly. By taking note of your boredom—in precisely the same way you just did with your excitement—you will gain clues about what your real research questions and problems might be.

Imagine a conversation between you and a well-meaning friend:

FRIEND: What are you working on?

YOU: Institutional sociology.

FRIEND: Ah, how interesting! I read an article the other day comparing the managerial structures of different companies, to see which ones created the most opportune conditions for workplace satisfaction and productivity.

YOU (TO YOURSELF): Wow, how painfully boring. That's not something I'm interested in studying at all.

Your friend rattles off more examples that, given your professed topic of interest, should in theory be of interest to you as well. They list the titles of books and summarize a few. The more you listen, the more confused you become. *Everything my friend is listing here is all so boring to me. Why? All these examples are clearly related to my topic, and so I guess I should be concerned with them. And yet I just don't care. What's wrong with me?*

A quiet terror begins to set in.

Maybe my topic is boring. Maybe I should switch topics. Or maybe this is just what research is like: a fleeting moment of excitement followed by the tedium of studying things you don't care about. Maybe I shouldn't do research!

Hold off on judging yourself (or your friend—they might actually be helping you!) and take a moment to reflect. Ask yourself: What about your chosen topic *bores* you? Among the potential questions or subtopics that derive quite naturally and obviously from your stated topic, which ones repel you, perhaps even unnerve you?

This might be the first time you've ever considered questions like these. After all, no one asks us what bores us. Everyone asks what *interests* or *excites* us. It's easy to see why answering questions about interests might lead us to learn something about ourselves that we might not know in a conscious way. But how would you explain why something *bores* you—especially something that seems like it should align with your topic of interest?

Here's what to do:

1. Go back to your search results, and scan them again.
2. Pay close attention to your EKG readout, focusing this time on the results that bore you. In the very same way that we spoke of not "outsmarting" yourself regarding your interests, you will need to be cautious during this process as well.
3. Choose a few "boring" results and write down answers to the same questions you answered before— this time for these different, *boring* search results:
   a. What does this make me think of?
   b. If I had to venture a guess, why did this one *not* jump out at me?
   c. What questions come to mind for me when I look at this search result?
4. Now, for each search result, write some version of this sentence: "I'm more interested in [something else] than [search result]."

Steps 3 and 4 produce two types of self-evidence that can give you detailed clues about the interior, unspoken, often unconscious mental makeup with which you are constantly making sense of the world.

Taking account of your boredom is part of your conversation with your research-self. Besides helping the process of elimination, steering you away from unprofitable lines of inquiry, boredom can also help you to ask better questions and zero in on your Problem.

- Denying boredom, or feigning interest in something because you feel it's "on topic" and demands your interest because it's "important."
- Engaging in circular logic. Don't fall prey to explanations that go something like this: "The reason this thing bores me is because it's boring!" Boredom is not something that "happens" to you. Boredom, like inspiration, is a dynamic process that happens *between* you and whatever it is you're interacting with. The sensation of boredom is the *by-product* of reactions between the substance that makes you you, and the substances of the reality you're encountering.

TRY THIS NOW: Go Small or Go Home
The goal: *To generate specific, fact-focused questions about your topic before you've done in-depth research. These will lead to bigger questions later on.*

You are now in a great position to start moving from a topic to questions. You have a set of notes about two things:

1. What you noticed about sources on a topic, and your best guesses as to why you noticed those things
2. What, among the "logical" or "obvious" aspects of your proposed topic, bored you and why

Using all of this as inspiration, try the following—as always, *in writing*.

In a stream of consciousness, write out a minimum of twenty questions related to your topic. The key is to make your questions *as specific as possible*, using the following prompts:

- What facts do you wish to know about your topic?
- Which data or information about your topic might you need to satisfy your curiosity?
- What telling details about your topic do you imagine might exist?

Some questions might be prompted by your initial contact with the sources you used in the "Search Yourself" exercise, or in "Let Boredom Be Your Guide." Others might be new.

Try to avoid posing questions that strive to be profound or too big-picture. If you find yourself asking questions about the essential "meaning" or "significance" of your topic, chances are you are thinking too abstractly.

Remember, too that *question means question*—with a question mark—and not a statement or sentence fragment masquerading as a question. "The question of justice" is not a question.

Again, your goal here is *not* to justify the significance of your project to someone else. You need to start with questions about basic facts. After all, you are new to your topic, and what you *don't* know about it far outweighs what you do.

An example: let's say you are looking at a black-and-white photograph taken during the proceedings of the military tribunals held in Nuremberg, Germany, in the wake of World War II. You might well wonder about big-picture questions, like "What effect did the trials at Nuremberg have on post–World War II Europe?" or "What was the significance of these trials?" But when you're trying to formulate a research project, it's the specific questions that will get you there faster:

> Which nations were represented at the trial?
> Who was sent as the delegate of each nation?
> How were the delegates chosen?
> What were their roles in the proceedings?
> Did anyone refuse to go?
> Who were the judges?
> How were they appointed?
> Who appointed them?
> Was this the first postwar tribunal of its kind?
> If not, where were the earlier ones?
> Were members of the media permitted to attend?
> Who took this photograph?
> How was the photo distributed, when, and by whom?
> In what building and what room did the proceedings take place?
> Did the trial proceed during one contiguous period of time—over the course of a few days, weeks, months—or were there different parts of the trial, spread out over time?
> Was there a deadline by which the trial had to conclude?
> Who created a transcript of the proceedings?
> Where was the transcript kept, or how was it distributed?
> Who paid for all of this?
> Who paid to transport judges, lawyers, and witnesses to the city?
> Who paid for their lodging, or for their lost wages?
> While standing trial, where, and for how long, were the accused parties incarcerated?

Notice that none of these questions is profound. They are small-scale and specific. Specificity is the goal at this point, for two reasons.

First, it is only through *small* questions like these that you can begin to form a picture in your mind (and in your notebook) about the core fundamentals of the topic you are researching. To try and answer "profound" questions at this point—about "meaning" and "significance"—is premature, since you don't yet have the facts, much less the opportunity, to analyze them. By contrast, the more facts you know about the physical space where the tribunal was held, or about the identities of the judges, lawyers, witnesses, onlookers, reporters, families, and others present, the greater command you begin to have of your subject matter. This, in turn, *prepares you for the process of asking "bigger" questions—"profound" questions—when the time is right.*

Second, lurking in one or more of those "small" questions may be an *unexpected* question that could, when you hear yourself ask it aloud, send your research off into an entirely new direction. For example: when asking a simple question like *Who paid for the lodging, food, and transportation costs of witnesses?* you might find yourself wanting to explore the history of international tribunals from a different perspective—not from the perspective of the courtroom drama itself, but, say, from the perspective of urban history, asking questions like *How did cities like Nuremberg, Tokyo, and Nanjing handle war crimes trials logistically? How did war-torn cities, whose infrastructures lay in ruins, handle transportation, housing, security, and more for such important events?*

Even from these few further questions, you can already see how you are moving toward a research project that might teach us something new and insightful about a grand topic like justice.

When you begin to ask (and then to answer) precise and seemingly mundane questions like these, you begin to liberate yourself from the confines of vague and un-productive "topics," moving instead toward specific and coherent clusters of questions that will, over time, add up to something compelling, open-ended, and doable.

Asking precise factual questions is one key to escaping Topic Land.

COMMONLY MADE MISTAKES
- Asking vague, grand, abstract, or big-picture questions about "meaning" or "significance," instead of specific and precise factual questions
- Not asking actual questions (with a question mark), but instead writing statements or sentence fragments—topics masquerading as questions
- Not asking a question because you think you couldn't answer it, perhaps because you think that the data doesn't exist or is unattainable
- Asking too few questions, resulting in an inadequate quantity of self-evidence

SOUNDING BOARD:
Start Building Your Research Network
You've done quite a bit of work by this point, all on your own. You've been thinking through topics and questions, and have done three exercises to generate new questions based on a topical interest.

Now's a good time to use the questions you've generated to start a conversation about research with someone you know. Start building your research network—a community of people you can consult with and seek advice from during the research process. Make a list of teachers, colleagues, students, and fellow travelers you think would be willing and available to discuss ideas with you on a periodic basis. Some researchers do a large portion of their research individually, but a reliable Sounding Board can be a catalyst.

Circle a couple of names on your list of potential Sounding Boards. Choose a few of the questions you've generated while reading this chapter, and make a meeting to discuss them. Keep things open-ended. You're not asking your Sounding Board to tell you which of your questions is "the best." Tell them you're not trying to settle on a research question just yet. You're in an exploratory stage. The goal is to get on their radar, and to start the process of communicating about your research ideas orally—since you've already done some writing.

You could send them your questions in advance, but strive to make it a casual conversation. Don't ask them "Are my questions *good*?" but "What do these questions make you think of?" and "What other questions do these questions make you ask?" Spend some time generating questions about a topic together.

And say *Thank you*. You may well be seeking them out again.

You Have Questions

You're now well on your way. You started with a general interest and identified an equally general "topic"— an object or focus of inquiry. You "searched yourself," generating a preliminary body of notes — self-evidence — based on an honest exploration of your attractions and repulsions. By writing about why certain things jumped out at you, and why others bored you, you've gained a clearer sense of your own standpoint and concerns, and you've used those exercises to generate specific and narrow questions. If your questions seem scattered, fragmentary, and chaotic, that's OK; in fact, that means you're doing things right. (If you have only a few questions, however, you should take another pass at the preceding exercise.)

Most importantly, in formulating these possible research questions, you've set aside for the time being any concerns about whether or not your questions are Important, with a capital *I*. We'll get to what other people think in part 2. Your list of questions contains questions that *matter to you, even if you don't know why yet*. As a bonus, you also have an initial set of primary and secondary sources from your database searches.

You have begun the process of transforming a topic into *questions*.

In the next chapter, we will show you how to analyze these questions to determine how they all connect. And once you connect them, you will discover that, underlying many if not all of these narrow and scattered questions, there resides something deeper that drives your work: your *Problem*.

For now, close this book, and give yourself time to recharge. We'll see you soon.

2. What's Your Problem?

Now that you have questions, the next step is to answer them, right?

Not exactly.

In this chapter, you will begin to find and use primary sources, and you may find the answers to at least some of your questions. But answering questions will not be the primary focus. *Educating* your questions will be the focus.

The questions you have generated thus far are, by and large, less developed than they could be and will become. This has nothing to do with your abilities as a researcher. Rather, it is a fundamental part of this stage of research: your questions are underdeveloped at this point because you have not yet had the chance to conduct research into your subject matter. It's to be expected.

Wait a minute! You might protest at this moment. *Before, you told me that I need to generate questions in order to do research. But now you're telling me that I need to do research in order to generate questions? That's impossible. It's an infinite loop. It's a trap!*

It's not a trap. But it is true that it takes a lot of research to arrive at the right questions. And then it takes *more* research to *answer* these questions and generate new ones. In this early stage of research, the goal is not, as many assume, the generation of answers. It is about the refinement of your existing questions and the generation of new (and better) ones.

The goal of this chapter is to help you identify and articulate the *problem* underlying your many research questions.

Accomplish this, and you will end up asking better questions, doing more significant research, and carrying it out more effectively.

Don't Jump to a Question
(or You'll Miss Your Problem)

Over the course of generating, analyzing, refining, and adding to your questions, you may have wondered: *How do I know when I've found my Problem? Do I really have a "Problem," or have I merely compiled a random set of questions that don't really add up to anything?* After all, we're curious about many things, but we don't launch research projects to satisfy every curiosity. Nor should we.

Here's a simple way to distinguish a *problem* from a random set of curiosities: if it changes by the day, week, or month, chances are it's a passing curiosity. If it endures, it just might be a problem.

A problem is a nagging presence within you — one that disturbs, bothers, and unsettles you, but also attracts, compels, and keeps you coming back. It's something that generates questions in your mind — questions that, no matter how varied and unrelated they might seem to an outsider, you know to be somehow interrelated, even if you can't explain why. A problem is something that follows you around. It doesn't care if you are a historian of France, a sociologist of the Philippines, or a literary scholar of India — it calls out for you to try to solve it. Your job is to give that problem a name, to identify a *case* of that problem that you will be able to study (given your personal abilities and constraints), and to figure out how to study that *case* so that you might arrive at a broader solution.

Researching a problem requires asking questions, of course, but (again, to state the obvious) a question is not a problem.

You can think of plenty of questions that have answers, but whose answers do not solve any problem. Asking and answering such idle questions is a waste of time, so *you want to make sure that your questions are indeed problem-driven.* This is why it is so important not to jump to a question.

A problem has several functions for the researcher, among them the following:

- It motivates you to ask questions about your topic.
- It determines which questions you ask.
- It defines the what/why/when/how of your engagement with your topic.
- It guides the path of your inquiry.
- It shapes the story you tell when the time comes to share your research results.

Up to now, you have been generating "first-draft" questions based on an initial foray into sources. But you want to make sure that you are asking questions that do more than just satisfy a personal curiosity. The next steps in this chapter will help you figure out

- how to *improve the questions* you have already generated;
- how to *use sources to identify the problem* motivating your questions;
- how to use your Problem to *generate new and better questions.*

We all know not to "jump to a conclusion"—an action prompted by prejudicial or hasty thought. We've all seen it happen, and we've all done it ourselves—we arrive at an argument or thesis about a sure thing even though we haven't spent sufficient time thinking it over. And we end up being wrong.

What the early-stage researcher has to avoid is jumping to a *question.* You have generated many questions, and the risk now is that you'll feel pressured to jump ahead and choose one prematurely.

What is your Research Question? You'll hear this demand from other people, and eventually from a little voice in your head that tries to trick you into thinking that your project must have only *one* Research Question, and that you must settle on it early.

The *Jump-to-a-Question Trap* can be as harmful as the Narrow-Down-Your-Topic Trap.

Jumping to a question is like constructing a home without examining the ground on which it will stand. Your architectural plan might be stunning, the plot of land spacious, and the vista marvelous, but if you build on sand you are going to have serious issues when those sands shift. By the time issues show up, renovations may be costly, and you might find it impossible to relocate.

Stress-Testing Your Questions

Now that you have done the work of producing a multitude of questions — small, factual questions, ideally — you will still need to stress-test, refine, and winnow them out, removing any dead ends, enhancing the rest, and adding additional questions that will better serve your research process.

Think of a question as if it were a car. Before jumping into this vehicle, and certainly before bringing others along, you would want assurance that its steering and brakes have been subjected to rigorous testing. You'd want to know that prototypes underwent crash tests, over and over, until the manufacturer felt certain that the structure of the vehicle was ideally suited to protect the driver and the passengers.

Here are two ways to stress-test your questions and improve their soundness. The first focuses on language; the second is subject-specific and focuses on sources. We recommend that you tackle them in that order.

Run a Diagnostic Test on Your Questions
The goal: *To ensure that the vocabulary, grammar, and phrasing of your questions are specific and unprejudiced so that they do not presume a certain outcome.*

Rewrite your research questions with particular attention to the following:

1. *Punctuation.* Do your questions actually end in a question mark? Or have you phrased them in more general, and vaguer, terms like "This is an examination of . . . ," "I plan to explore . . . ," or "My project is about the question of . . . "? If you find yourself articulating your questions as "I want to examine how" something happened, there is a fair chance that what you have are not really questions at all, but rather *topics disguised as questions*. Be more specific, and add a question mark.

2. *Adjectives and adverbs.* Do your questions rely on broad, generic, imprecise, or sweeping adjectives like "modern," "traditional," or "Western," or adverbs like "scientifically," "rationally," or "effectively"? Try to cut such adjectives and adverbs out entirely.

3. *Collective nouns.* Do your questions depend upon collective nouns like "Asians," "the French," "students," "women," or "North Americans"? If so, do your best to replace these nouns with more precise demographic categories: *women of what ages, students living where and when, North Americans of what background, socioeconomic status, race or ethnicity, or family status?* You do not need to take into account *all* possible demographic variables, but you do want to try to include all of those that might make a difference to your project.

4. *Verbs*. Do your questions contain verbs like "influence," "affect," "shape," or "impact" or passive constructions such as "was affected by," "responded to," or "reacted to"? In such cases, chances are high that you are building your questions in such a way that they rule out an entire set of possible answers and outcomes. Rephrase to avoid presumptions that could result in confirmation bias.

By the end of this process, your questions should meet these criteria:

- *They should be clear, precise, and jargon-free.* If your questions are too hard for a colleague or mentor to understand, this means that *you* (and not they) still don't get what your Problem really is. Your shorthand might be hiding your significant specifics. Likewise, if your Problem is hiding behind jargon—words designed to make your questions sound "smart" and "important"—replace it with language that is clear and *vulnerable*. You and your intended audience should be able to tell what your research is driving at, even if this means your language might be less articulate and refined— and less concise—than you might like.
- *They should be rooted in verifiable and falsifiable data.* Your research questions should have integrity. This means that they should be inspired by fact, rather than by speculation, prejudice, or opinion. What are the facts that motivated these questions? Are they verifiable? Where and how could these facts be checked? Have you checked them yourself?
- *They should be indifferent to the outcome.* The

best research questions are open, agnostic, unprejudiced. Put another way, a research question should not presume a certain answer. If yours does, rewrite it to eliminate that presumption.

- *They should be clear about the subject.* Your questions should not be reliant on broad categories of identity, such as "students," "women," "Europeans," "Brazilians," "Christians," and so on. Refer to the suggestions above, and be as specific as you can be about the *who* in your question.

- *They should be raw and undisciplined.* At least for now. Although we encourage you to make sure that each *individual* question in your list is as precise, detailed, and grounded as possible, remember that, collectively, your list of questions need not be overly polished or coherent at this point. If the questions seem random to you, *let them be random*. If they seem unrelated to one another, *let them be unrelated*.

COMMONLY MADE MISTAKES

- Asking *leading questions*, which are phrased so as to predetermine the answer. These questions are motivated by unproven assumptions, and result in confirmation bias. The result of leading questions is that you inevitably find what you are looking for. (See the example below of *How did X influence Y?*)

- Asking *advocacy questions*, which promote a certain ideology (taken-for-granted worldview) or course of action. These questions take a position and encourage others to adopt it, irrespective of the actual facts of the case or which interpretations the evidence suggests are plausible. Example: "Why is 'feminism' a better analytical rubric than 'romance' for understanding Joan Didion's novels?"

- Forcing all your questions to "make sense" or "add up." Don't worry. That part will come soon.

Leading questions are so common and so prejudicial to the research process that it's worth looking at one extended example. Maybe you've seen a version of this question before:

How did X affect Y?

Consider this example:

How did the ruinous taxation policies of King Louis XVI during the 1780s erode popular support for the aristocracy and pave the way for the French Revolution?

Wow, that is one "educated" question! In order to pose it in the first place, one would already need to know a considerable amount about French history.

But take another look. See any issues? When we ask *How did X affect Y?* the implied answer is that X *did* affect Y, and all that remains are questions of *how* and *to what degree*. Building a question this way creates a major weakness. The researcher at this point has not yet established that such influence existed in the first place. The very phrasing of the question rules out the possibility that X *didn't* affect Y at all. If it turns out that it didn't, you'd have one heck of a short paper.

Let's say your hunch is still that X *did* affect Y. It might have. However, you couldn't know at this point, having not yet done the research. What you want to avoid is building your questions in such a way that you actually *need* this "influence" to exist in order for your questions to be viable. Almost inevitably, you will end up discovering spe-cious "proof" of influence in primary source material, mis-leading both your readers and yourself.

If you detect shortcomings in your question, try to re-pair them. If your question is actually a topic masquerad-ing as a question, reword or restructure it. If you are rely-ing on abstract nouns, adjectives, or adverbs, substitute specific words. Articulate your question without using any sweeping words at all. And if your choice of verbs is com-mitting you to research outcomes too early, change them.

TRY THIS NOW:
Use Primary Sources to Educate Your Questions
The goal: *To learn how to run keyword searches designed to enhance or "educate" the questions you are asking about your topic. These searches uncover primary sources relevant to your research that themselves contain new keywords you were previously unaware of (thereby enabling you to run follow-up searches to reveal even more, and more use-ful, primary sources).*

Running language diagnostics like you did in the pre-vious exercise is a first step that will help you avoid com-mon errors when posing your questions. This next exercise requires you to delve back into your specific subject mat-ter and into primary sources.

Thus far, we've been keeping you somewhat at arm's length from primary sources. In chapter 1, we specifically encouraged you *not* to delve into them too deeply in the "Search Yourself" exercise. We now encourage you to dive in, but in ways you might not expect. Rather than trying to use primary sources to start answering the questions you've come up with, we want you to use them to develop, refine, and expand those questions. You'll eventually start using primary sources to answer questions, but at this early stage, we suspect, your questions still need more refinement before you start investing large amounts of time and energy in answering them.

How do we use primary sources to strengthen and "educate" our questions? The answer is simple: primary sources alert you the existence of *other* primary sources, exposure to which helps you ask more mature questions about your subject. By contrast, researchers who "jump to questions," and then dive headlong into answering those questions using primary sources, run the risk of confining themselves to a kind of intellectual and empirical bubble.

Let's imagine that you're interested in one of the following topics:

- turn-of-the-twentieth-century African American literature
- the history of artificial intelligence
- food culture in twentieth-century Hong Kong

Let's further imagine that you've already done the hard work of transforming your initial topic into a set of specific questions, and that you're now collecting and exploring sources. You start by running searches in a digital repository of historic newspapers containing hundreds of fully text-searchable periodicals from across the world.

But then you hit a stumbling block. Practically all the search results for "*food AND Hong Kong*" come from the 1950s onward. Or a search for "*African American AND literature*" yields many articles and reports from the 1980s onward, but almost nothing from earlier periods. A search for "artificial intelligence" returns lots of materials from the 1980s onward, but very little before.

What is going on? Common sense tells you that there

were African American writers circa 1900, that food culture in Hong Kong predates the 1950s, and that research into AI began before the 1980s. Why is your search failing?

In this case, the cause is simple: the keywords you're using are anachronistic. That is to say, these are terms that people use *here* (in your hypothetical location) and *now* to describe the identities, places, and subjects you are trying to find primary sources about. But these are *not* the words that people necessarily used in the past, or in other places. "Artificial intelligence" is a term *we use today* to describe a branch of computer science. *It isn't necessarily the one used by the scientists who gave rise to this field.* They more often used terms like "Systems Thinking," "Machine Intelligence," and a number of others. As a place-name, "Hong Kong" has been in usage for a very long time, and yet *as an English-language spelling*, it has changed a great deal (decades ago, you would have been much more likely to see it spelled "Hong-Kong," with a hyphen, or "Hongkong," as one word). Likewise, the term "African American" was popularized only in the 1980s, prior to which one would have encountered terms like "Afro-American," "Negro," "Colored," and other appellations, many of which are deeply offensive today.

In this earliest stage of finding primary sources, then, your main goal is actually *not* to start answering your questions, but to use the primary sources you do find to reveal *new* keywords that you did not know existed—keywords that you can then feed back into the search process, in order to uncover *more and better primary sources*, *more and better keywords*, and most importantly of all, *more and better questions*.

This may seem like a daunting recommendation. After all, even if your search terms are "imperfect," they may return thousands—even tens of thousands—of results.

Should you *really* be expected to read, notate, and cite even *more* sources?

Not necessarily. And fear not—we'll get to source management. Right now, your goal is to identify omissions in your search inputs, so as to eliminate false negatives in those searches' outputs. Big picture, you're improving your grasp of your topic by eliminating blind spots.

Whenever you do a keyword search, ask yourself: *Are there other search terms I should be using? Might there be different spellings of the search terms I already have?* You need to be as confident as possible that the search results you are getting are broadly representative and reflective of available primary sources, and not the by-product of narrow or unrefined searches. If your search results all cluster within a narrow time period (as in our example) or were produced in a very small number of places or were written by a very small number of people, chances are that something in your search process is the cause. Phrased differently: Hong Kong existed before the 1950s, as did African American writers before the 1980s, and so the peculiar clustering of your results has nothing to do with "reality" at large, and everything to do with the *way you searched*. And if you didn't stop to refine your search, instead racing ahead to read, notate, and cite all of the materials you did find, your overall research project would be woefully incomplete.

Here are some techniques to help you use primary sources to refine your keyword searches.

The Art and Science of Keyword Search: A Few Tricks

Improving a keyword search might sound like a rather straightforward process, but there is a devilish paradox at play: most of the primary sources you discover that contain "present-day keywords" (e.g., "artificial intelligence," "African American," "Hong Kong," . . .) will *not contain the other keywords that you need to find* ("Hong-kong," "Hongkong," "Afro-American," . . .). In most searches, the situation is all-or-nothing. Either the keyword you used in your search is present in the primary source, and thus the source appears in your search results; or the keyword is not there, and it simply doesn't. Here's how to get around that impasse.

Take Advantage of Category Searches

In certain databases, you might be fortunate to come across materials that are accompanied by *metadata* (data about data), crafted by librarians and archivists whose goal it is to make sources more discoverable to researchers like you. In such cases, you might find a primary source that contains the term "artificial intelligence," and then discover that it has also been "tagged" with this same keyword in the database. By clicking on this tag, you gain access to all of the *other* primary sources in that database that were categorized that way—including those that may not contain the term "artificial intelligence" at all! This is one way to get from a source that contains *only* the keywords you used in your search to another source that contains *none* of the keywords you used.

Here's what to do: after you run your search, and receive your results, sort the results chronologically, and then explore only the results that come *before* the 1980s—the time when, in your preliminary search, they seemed to disappear. As you scan through these titles, take notice: What words show up in the title? If you are able to read the work online, scan the table of contents, the preface, the introduction, and the index. What words, terms, and vocabulary are used? Are there any words or phrases you notice that might, if you were to run them through your database search, yield other hits that your first keyword search did not? *These are your new keywords. Write them down.*

A caveat: metadata, too, is the product of context and should not be taken as definitive. Categories are cultural constructs, including those created by librarians and archivists. The categories in the metadata they create are shaped by stances and worldviews and protocols, and thus should never be taken as the "final word" on any subject. Always assume there is more, and that no one can do your work for you.

Locate Self-Reflexive Sources

In some cases, you might be fortunate to find a primary source, like a historical dictionary, that explicitly addresses the shifting nomenclature surrounding the very topic the primary source is about, outlining for you the varied ways a given idea, place, community, practice, or the like has been named and renamed across time and space. Moments like this are joyous, since they open countless doors that the researcher need only walk through!

Even in such cases, however, remember that a primary source still is subject to its own limitations. No source will document all of the variants in terminology that might be useful to your searches. No source (as we explain below) should be taken as the final word on the subject. It still falls to you to determine whether or not the primary source in question is empirically accurate. Every source possesses its own stances, worldviews, and perspectives. But for your current purpose of finding more generative keywords, the source can be useful to you whether or not its data or conclusions are accurate, so you can defer judgment on those questions for the time being. The goal for now is to determine if this source will lead you in the direction of further primary sources that you wouldn't have been able to find otherwise.

Keep Track of Your Keywords and Searches

As you discover and try out more and more keywords—and even a smaller-scale project can produce hundreds—it's easy to lose track of them and get overwhelmed. The other fundamental aspect of this process involves, alas, the unglamorous world of record-keeping.

Did I try this keyword before? I can't remember. Did I try this keyword in this database? Not sure. When was the last time I ran this keyword in this database? No idea.

The dangers of missing something are real, since databases are continually updated and expanded, and since some projects can take many months—or years—to complete. You can imagine how many hours you might end up wasting repeating searches you've already done.

Fortunately, there's a simple solution: track your searches using a table. Here's how, in three steps:

1. In the rows on the left side, enter the keywords you plan to use.
2. In the column headers, enter all of the electronic databases or library catalogues you plan to explore.
3. Inside each cell, keep track of when you ran a particular search. Enter the date of your search, and perhaps also a brief note on the number of results you found.

The result is a huge time-saver, and better research results: you will always know, at a glance, which searches you have run, or still need to.

TABLE 2. TRACK YOUR KEYWORD SEARCHES

	Database 1	Database 2	⋮	⋮	Add columns as needed.
Keyword 1	☐	☑ 9/30/20			
Keyword 2	☑ 9/27/20	☐			
...					
...					
...					
...					
Add rows as needed.					

For more keyword search tips, tracking sheets, and a downloadable version of table 2, visit whereresearchbegins.com.

As you continue to use primary sources to further "educate" your questions, two other helpful things will inevitably happen: you will end up *answering* some of your questions along the way, and you will find that some are not actually worth answering. In other words, you will discover that some of your initial questions can be scrapped. This is precisely what you want to happen.

The process can feel miraculous. As you stress-test your questions, you learn more about your subject matter. And as you learn more, your *instincts* regarding your subject matter improve. In "educating your questions" you are educating your instincts. When an experienced mechanic tells you, "Sounds like something's wrong with your transmission," you listen closely because their ability to detect anomalies is highly refined. To the average car owner, any loud noise might prompt us to ask the generic question "What's wrong?" Educating your questions will help you to hone in on "real" questions, and you'll happily discard the ones born of naivete.

TRY THIS NOW: Make Your Assumptions Visible
The goal: *To become aware of the assumptions you bring to your research project and use them to identify the problem that motivates your research questions.*

Now that you've analyzed your questions using the two techniques described above, there is still one more thing you need to do: identify the assumptions that underlie your questions, make them visible, and make peace with them.

You are not a blank slate. You arrived at your topic and your questions with a whole mess of assumptions. This is a natural thing—a good thing, in fact. After all, these are the reasons why you *thought* the topic is interesting and why you *think* your question is the right one for you. Everyone brings their own baggage to a research project.

Welcome to Baggage Claim.

Some teachers take it as their mission to "shatter" all your "illusions" about the world.

You believe the Vikings were a horde of marauding savages? Behold as I tear the veil of ignorance from your eyes!

You believe that Japanese society is homogenous? Watch as I reduce your prejudicial views to dust!

Dispelling misconceptions can be useful in many pedagogical and research settings. Yet the dispelling process, however well meaning, can have an inhibitory effect. Watching a fellow researcher or student get "disabused" can make others want to keep quiet to avoid being embarrassed themselves. For the researcher, the "disabuse" model can also lead to the unproductive belief that assumptions are the *enemy*—that they are shameful things to keep hidden, obstacles to be overcome, or evidence of incompetence.

Self-Centered Research is premised upon a very different approach to assumptions, as follows:

1. Assumptions should be made visible, and thus vulnerable.
2. Assumptions should not, however, be stigmatized, silenced, or driven underground, since this, counterintuitively, encourages *holding on to them more tightly*.
3. Assumptions are *fuel* to be consumed. Using them, you can achieve two goals at once: you can move in a new direction, and you can exhaust your assumptions in the process (meaning that you will eventually need *new* fuel).

Your assumptions about the world—even the most naive or negative—*serve you* at this point in the research process. To set out on a research quest with no assumptions at all would be like trying to sail on a windless day. Assumptions are the wind in your sails, and you need to channel them to keep your voyage on course.

Before evaluating your assumptions—which you will do shortly—thank them for helping you take note of things. They are the reason that any search results jumped out at you at all. They are what helped you notice a detail in a primary source. *It was the gaps between your assumptions and the world as it really is that gave rise to all those specific research questions*. Your assumptions shape your *expectations* about reality. And when those expectations are *not* met, it's time to pay attention.

So let's get to work on making your assumptions visible, and vulnerable. Here's what to do:

1. Review your most recent set of questions and ask yourself: For each of these questions, what has to be true *in advance* in order for me to ask this question in the first place?
2. List the small questions/things you noticed, and write down the assumptions you may hold that helped you notice each in the first place.
3. Make a list of the assumptions you bring to this particular question, and sort them into the following categories:
   a. Assumptions you want to work with, for now
   b. Assumptions you want to discard right away
   c. Assumptions you are unsure or ambivalent about
4. Write two lines to justify your choice for putting each assumption in a particular category.
5. Now go back to all of the questions in your list whose underlying assumptions fall into category A. Since these are built on assumptions that you, having reflected on them, feel safe in maintaining, then these questions are good as they are.
6. What about questions whose underlying assumptions fall into category B? Although you might be tempted to, *do not throw them away just yet!* If you find them to be based on weak, prejudicial, or unfounded assumptions, try to rephrase them so that they aren't. Can they be rebuilt as more grounded, open-ended questions? Try to improve them before you discard them.
7. As for questions built on category C assumptions, these fall somewhere in between. Most likely you would want to keep them in your list, but perhaps

flag them, as reminders to yourself that you want to keep an eye on them, and revisit them as your research deepens.

To keep things organized, try creating a chart like the one in table 3 for each question, in which you identify and analyze underlying assumptions and revise the question as needed.

TABLE 3. MAKE YOUR ASSUMPTIONS VISIBLE

RESEARCH QUESTION:		
Assumption (one-sentence description)	Category (A / B / C)	Why did I put this assumption in this category? (two-sentence explanation)
Revised research question:		

Here's an example: Imagine that one of the things you noticed and wrote down was a short quotation that jumped out at you in a letter written between two friends in the year 1944, during World War II. Perhaps there was a particular passage or sentence that jumped out at you—perhaps one of the friends cracked a joke about the war, and it stuck with you.

In this exercise, it's your goal to brainstorm *why* the passage or sentence jumped out at you, by contemplating what assumptions you may hold that this quote contradicted. Feel free to speculate. You are not expected to "know yourself completely" right away—that takes time. Perhaps you think that people living during World War II would never have dreamed about making jokes about a conflict that, by the year 1944, had already taken the lives of millions and destroyed the lives of countless more. Or perhaps you assume that, during wartime in general, people are allergic to humor itself, and prefer to carry themselves in a somber manner befitting the gravity of their situation. Or perhaps you assume that there are some episodes and experiences in history that are so horrific—the Holocaust, the Armenian Genocide, the slave trade—that no one would dream of speaking about them comically.

Write down every possible reason why you might think what you think, even if you're uncertain, without judging them as good or bad. The point here is not to "expose" your assumptions in a negative way. Rather, the goal is to bring to the surface those parts of your thinking that remain invisible yet influence how you think.

COMMONLY MADE MISTAKES
- Not identifying or divulging the assumptions motivating your research questions—for any reason, including embarrassment or self-consciousness. Remember: you're admitting these assumptions to yourself so that you can improve your own thinking. There is no external judgment here.
- Not attempting to revise or restructure a research question based on category B assumptions.
- Dismissing or throwing out category C assumptions, instead of examining them as a type of self-evidence. Remember: the gaps between your assumptions and the world as it really is can generate useful research questions.

TRY THIS NOW:

Identify the Problem That Connects Your Questions

The goal: *To identify the problem underlying your multiple draft research questions.*

Now you're ready to take a key step. In chapter 1 you "searched yourself" to find questions within a topic. Now you'll search yourself again, but this time with more self-evidence. By now, you have completed several exercises to produce a large number of questions about facts related to your project. What you now want to figure out is, What is the problem that connects your questions?

Try to think flexibly but rigorously. What relationships can you find between the different questions and fragments you have created and gathered thus far? What motivates your search for these particular facts? You could have asked any questions about this topic—why *these*? Which questions are the most compelling to you (and which seem less important)? Figure this out, and you'll have accomplished a major breakthrough: you'll have identified the underlying pattern that connects all (or most) of your questions in a coherent whole. In other words, you will have found your Problem.

Try this procedure:

1. Lay all of your questions out in front of you.
2. Do not try to answer all those questions for now. Instead, ask yourself: What are the shared concerns that connect these questions?
3. Step outside yourself. If you were someone else looking at these questions, what might you speculate are the deeper questions that connect these small questions?
4. Write down those questions.
5. If necessary, prioritize your questions by degree of specificity or generality, as medium-level or high-

level questions. These questions should be more general than the specific factual questions you generated earlier.

The higher-level questions might not all add up. Don't force them to. But be creative, and spend some time on this. What are the parent categories that connect two or more of your questions? The connective tissue might not be obvious immediately. Finding it might require thinking counterintuitively.

COMMONLY MADE MISTAKES
- Trying to answer your multiple questions, instead of focusing on identifying the shared concern that underlies them.
- Not thinking beyond the particular topic or case, and ignoring a more fundamental concern.

SOUNDING BOARD: Get Leads on Primary Sources
When you are searching for your Problem, or verifying that the problem you've been working with is the right one for you, it might still be too early to talk to a Sounding Board about your assumptions. As we mentioned above, the tendency of experts and authorities to "disabuse" us of "bad" assumptions is so prevalent that you will probably want to delay that conversation for the time being.

What your Sounding Board *can* help you with at this stage is finding primary sources that you can use to educate your questions. Above, we've provided a few examples of databases you can use for the exercises in this chapter. Describe those exercises to your Sounding Board, and ask for suggestions of other databases or archive catalogues or repositories of primary sources you might use.

You Have a Problem (in a Good Way)

You have now taken a close look at your many factual questions and grouped them under parent categories by shared concern. You have formulated higher-level questions motivated by these concerns. The key concern that overshadows all others might have emerged in a flash or intuition. Or perhaps you're still trying to decide which of them is the most important to you. If you feel like you don't yet have enough self-evidence, you can of course repeat the exercises in this chapter. But even if you think you do, you might still wonder: How do I know when I've truly discovered my Problem?

A problem is never a fleeting thing. Rather, it is something that is sustained and enduring. To you, it can't be easily dismissed or ignored. Frida Kahlo painted surrealistic self-portraits because she was driven by a *problem*. In the world of music, John Coltrane worked on *A Love Supreme*, and Billie Holiday sang "Strange Fruit" because they were driven by problems. Bob Dylan entered a "blue period" because of a problem. Researchers are just the same.

Problems are good things. They are good to have, good to worry about, good to mull over. The problems we carry around with us can be thought of as the productive frictions that happen as we move through, and rub up against, existence itself.

Ultimately, however, the final decision can only come from you. Only you can know whether or not the cluster of fascinating questions you've generated thus far add up to a problem, or just a highly sophisticated and interesting set of curiosities.

You may well have multiple problems, but for now let's just tackle one problem at a time. We'll discuss what to do with the others in the final chapter.

3. Designing a Project That Works

· ·

Having arrived at a problem, now you must make decisions about what you can accomplish, given your available resources. In particular, you need to think about the primary sources you'll need to answer your questions and solve your Problem, as well as the resources you'll need (including time!) to put together a project.

The issues this chapter deals with are both conceptual and practical: What are primary sources? Which ones can you actually access? How can you discover the full potential of a source related to your topic, or look beyond the obvious questions one might ask about a source to arrive at something original? How can you use such sources to pinpoint your Problem? What arguments can you make with your sources? How many sources can you acquire? How much time will you have to analyze them? How should you design your project, given your personal work habits, material constraints, or deadline?

Getting from a problem to a project involves more than just logistics. Project planning involves self-assessment and visualization. What model or type of project is most suitable for you? What do you want the finished product to look like?

Primary Sources and How to Use Them (or, Fifty Ways to Read a Cereal Box)

Sources are essential to original research, so figuring out how to identify, evaluate, and use them is a crucial practical consideration. Researchers conventionally divide sources into two general categories: primary sources and secondary sources. Research guides typically define *primary sources* as "original" or "raw" materials. They are the evidence that you use to develop and test claims, hypotheses, and theories about reality. Primary sources vary based on one's field of study. For historians, primary sources tend to date to the period of focus, whether they are written documents, like letters and maps, or any other type of physical object. Anthropologists might rely on oral testimony, or audio recordings. In fields such as literature or philosophy, primary sources are usually texts.

Most research guides define *secondary sources* along similar lines. *The Craft of Research* (4th edition) defines them as "books, articles, or reports that are based on primary sources and are intended for scholarly or professional audiences," and which researchers use to "keep up with developments in their fields" and to "frame new problems" by "challeng[ing] or build[ing] on the conclusions or methods of others" (p. 66).

While we largely agree with these definitions, we also want to reinforce a point well known to veteran researchers about the dangers of defining "primary" and "secondary" sources in terms of *absolutes*. We would advocate *not* thinking of primary sources solely as old objects or documents found in archives or online repositories, and secondary sources as studies that "use" primary sources the way one might process raw materials into finished products (to extend the above metaphor). If the term *primary sources* conjures up images of weathered manuscripts, sepia-toned photographs, shards of ancient pottery, or clippings from a centuries-old newspaper, it's time for a shift in perspective.

Absolutist definitions of sources get in the way of the process of identifying primary sources and asking research questions, for two reasons:

1. Any source can be *primary, secondary,* or *not a source for your project.*
2. A source's type is determined solely by its relationship with the questions you are trying to answer, and the problem you are trying to solve. A source is never inherently primary or secondary.

A more accurate definition of *primary source* would be the following: a source that is primary with respect to a particular question.

Notice how our definition recasts the "primary-ness" of a given source in relative terms.

Take, for example, a college-level US history textbook published in 2019. According to an absolutist definition of sources, there can be little doubt that this is not a "primary" source, since it draws on multiple works of scholarship. Someone who wants to learn about the First Continental Congress or the root causes of the American Civil War would refer to this book not as a primary source produced contemporaneously with the events in question, but as a secondary source that synthesizes historical arguments based upon sources, both primary and secondary.

But what if their question was not about the First Continental Congress directly, or about the causes of the Civil War, but about the *history of textbooks themselves,* or the *history of how the American Civil War has been presented in American higher education in the twentieth and twenty-first centuries*? What kind of source is this 2019 book now? Suddenly, a book that by all accounts should be considered "absolutely secondary" has become "primary," despite the fact that it was published recently. Under these circumstances, this book from 2019 would show up in your bibliography amid other relevant primary sources: perhaps college textbooks from 1905, 1923, 1945, and so forth. Perhaps you might have access to the personal papers of the textbook author, or the possibility of interviewing the scholars and editors who were responsible for the 2019 work. Perhaps you might have uncovered a repository of course syllabi from a single university, which would enable you to examine the ways in which university courses explained the Civil War during, say, the immediate aftermath of World War I, or the lead-up to World War II, or during the height of the civil rights movement.

Let's take this one step further. Just as the same source can be "primary" or "secondary," depending upon context, so too can the same source be "primary" in dramatically different ways. The very same source can show up in the bibliographies of strikingly different research projects, and can be used by different authors to pose dramatically different kinds of questions.

Imagine that, in your database searches, you encounter a cereal box from the 1960s.

You're not sure why this particular image intrigues you, but as you know well by now, "not knowing why" is entirely OK. Somehow, this source feels "primary" to your research interests, and so you trust your instinct and set out to figure out what questions it might help you answer.

Here you face a decision: how you treat this source will lead you down either a narrow path or a broad avenue of potential research questions.

The narrow route is to jump to the obvious candidates: questions about food culture, or perhaps about advertising or consumer culture. *After all,* you think to yourself, *this is a box of cereal, and so the questions we would want to ask should obviously pertain to things like food, right?*

You're thinking yourself into, well, a box.

Remember: as a *primary source,* a box of cereal can be "primary with respect to" countless questions that have *nothing to do with food per se.* Let's consider for a moment all of the different ways that a researcher could "read" a box of cereal. Or, to put this differently, let's brainstorm for a moment different kinds of research projects that might conceivably include this source—a 1960s cereal box—in a bibliography or list of sources.

Let's even go one step further and brainstorm what *other* primary sources this cereal box might end up "working alongside," depending upon the particular research project in which it appears.

Based on what we come up with, let's then give a name to the *genre* of questions we're asking, on the assumption that it might be connected to an underlying problem.

The rows in the table 4, while numerous, offer only a sample of the different directions one's research could take based on a single primary source. The key here is that when a source is unquestionably "primary," the question still remains, Primary *how*?

Mastering this method of dealing with primary sources will enhance the originality of your research. You will never

TABLE 4. THE CEREAL BOX CHALLENGE: HOW TO QUESTION PRIMARY SOURCES

What I notice about the source	Questions/concerns I might have	The very next primary source I might want to find	Broader subjects and/or genres of questions that might be related to my problem
The various codes found on the box (e.g., printing codes, shipment codes, or for later cereal boxes, bar codes)	Who uses these codes? Why are they positioned where they are on the box? How are they read or decoded? When did cereal boxes start to have such codes?	Materials related to laser scanning and its application to logistics (consumer, transportation, postal system, etc.)	Technology Supply chain logistics History
The "Nutritional Facts and Recommendations" on the side of the box	How are these facts and recommendations generated? By whom?	Early medical and public health treatises on recommended daily food intake, materials on the discovery/invention of the concept of the calorie	Biopolitics Standard measurements of energy and nutrition Government-industry relations
The "storytelling" one often finds on the back of the box	What did the producers or consumers of this product want it to say about the world? About consumers? About the company? Have the stories appearing on the backs of cereal boxes changed much over time? How about by type of cereal (e.g., sugar cereal vs. "healthy" cereal)?	Other kinds of consumer packaging in which stories are told (children's toys, exercise equipment, health and beauty products, etc.)	Stories, narratives, discourses Times: Future and past
The shape, size, and dimensions of the box	Why does the box have this weight and size, when assembled or pre-assembled? Where is the box stored or held? at various stages of the delivery process, and for how long at each stage? How does it get from where it was made to where it was intended to go? How many boxes are in a shipment?	Materials connected to the early history of containerized shipping	Transportation Logistics Global capitalism

TABLE 4. (*continued*)

What I notice about the source	Questions/concerns I might have	The very next primary source I might want to find	Broader subjects and/or genres of questions that might be related to my problem
The typefaces used on the packaging	Why are some typefaces larger than others? How were the fonts chosen? Which possibilities were considered and rejected?	Sample printed matter using low-cost, mass-produced paper stock, like telephone books, tabloid newspapers, psychological warfare pamphlets, etc.	Typography Design history Hierarchies of design
The color palette and symbols used on the package	What are the primary considerations influencing the color palette? What do the symbols on the box represent?	An advertising agency's internal report on how colors affect consumer behavior, circa 1960s Other products made by the same company	The psychology of color
The 4-color printing guide hidden under the top flap	Why is this design element positioned so that it cannot be seen in the store? Why is it on the box? How is it used? What other design elements are meant to be "invisible" to the consumer?	Other consumer products or food products containing hidden designs on the packaging	Machine-driven design Invisibility
The "Best If Used By" date	How is the expiration date calculated, and by whom? Does it appear on boxes of this cereal distributed in other countries?	FDA regulations on food expiry calculations and consumer notifications	Food safety Government regulatory regimes (national/international)
The paper or cardstock used to make the box itself	Which type(s) of tree is used to make the paper/cardstock? Where was it produced? How many trees per year were used to package this product? Is this (still) the industry standard?	Other material objects produced using wood- and wood-pulp-based products	Environmental history Forestry

(*continued*)

TABLE 4. (*continued*)

What I notice about the source	Questions/concerns I might have	The very next primary source I might want to find	Broader subjects and/or genres of questions that might be related to my problem
The glue used to seal the box, and the interior pouch	What substance is the glue made from? Who made it? How was the adhesive chosen? How do most consumers open it? How much of the product do the producers expect to go bad before it can be consumed?	Company R&D records on consumer habits Contracts with packaging vendors	Chemistry
The tab used to close or open the box	How would the box be used? Which designs were considered but rejected?	Other food products requiring repeated unsealing and resealing	Durability Utility
The archival box or container in which the cereal box is preserved	How and why did this box come to be preserved? Who preserved it? How? Where? Was it preserved by accident, or intentionally for some specific purpose?	Programs from annual meetings of the Society of American Archivists	Archiving Determinations of cultural/historical worth Museology
The price tag	How much did this box of cereal cost? How and where was the price advertised? Was the box of cereal cheap, of average cost, or expensive for US consumers in the 1960s? What was the item's availability? How did the price compare to the production and distribution costs? How much profit went to the producer versus the wholesaler versus the retailer?	Archives of historical grocery stores and food producers that enable one to chart fluctuations in the cost of basic consumer goods	Economic history Demographics Pricing strategies

again take a primary source at face value, or fall into the trap of asking only obvious questions. You'll always be thinking "outside the cereal box."

TRY THIS NOW:
Treat Your Primary Source Like a Cereal Box

The goal: *To adopt the habit of asking multiple genres of questions about each of your primary sources so as to identify problems that are not self-evident and thus might easily be overlooked. This technique will both enable you to decide which problem interests you most, and enhance your ability to conduct original research.*

Now it's your turn to take what we call the *Cereal Box Challenge.*

Using the search techniques you learned in chapters 1 and 2, track down and obtain a single source. The source should exert an unmistakable magnetism for you—it should be a source that you instinctively feel must be "primary" with regard to your emerging research concerns.

Using table 5 as your guide, take notice of as many different features of your source as possible. Disaggregate the source into its different elements, just as we did with the cereal box. Identify as many elements as possible, but no fewer than ten. Don't let yourself off the hook. If you don't find the equivalent of a UPC symbol, or a bar code, there might be other features of your source that connect it in some way to a broader system or standardization scheme. There might not be an allergy warning or a table of nutritional recommendations, but there is a high likelihood that the source is "caught up" in broader political, economic, sociocultural, or other discourses of concern to you. You will need to abstract and extrapolate from the cereal box example, because your source will likely not possess most of the *specific* features of that particular source.

As you fill in the first column, try to imagine the kinds of questions that could be asked by focusing on one or another specific feature of your source. Think expansively. Push your mind. Don't settle. If all of your "potential questions" are all about . . . well . . . *cereal* then you know you're not thinking hard enough. If you let your mind relax and commit to this exercise, you will quickly begin to ask questions that, proverbially speaking, get you from breakfast cereal to lasers in a single step. Add these questions to column 2.

Now imagine what a potential "very next source" might be for each of these feature-question pairings, and fill in column 3. Again, don't settle. Surprise yourself. Whatever you assume is too extreme is likely not.

Finally, return to your increasingly skilled faculties of introspection, asking yourself:

- Which of these feature-question-source#2 triad(s) lights my fire?
- Which excites me the most? Why, if I had to venture a guess?
- Which of these bore me? Why, if I had to venture a guess?
- What does this suggest about what my primary concerns might be?
- *How* is this source "primary" with respect to my questions and concerns?

Write all of this down.

TABLE 5. TREAT YOUR PRIMARY SOURCES LIKE A CEREAL BOX

What I notice about the source	Questions/ concerns I might have	The very next primary source I might want to find	Genres of questions that might be related to my Problem

COMMONLY MADE MISTAKES

- Asking only obvious or self-evident questions related to the ostensible topic of the source, instead of multiple *genres* of questions
- Asking questions that are vague and general instead of specific and factual
- Asking too few *genres* of questions—aim for at least ten. Err on the side of being creative, even far-fetched
- For "the very next primary source I might want to find," thinking only of sources within your Field (like food history, for a 1960s cereal box; for more on Fields, see chapter 5)
- After completing the table of noticings, questions, next sources, and genres of questions, skipping the steps of (a) gauging your relative interest in those results, and (b) writing down the result

TRY THIS NOW: Envision Your Primary Sources
The goal: *To identify places you might not have originally considered looking for primary sources. This will enhance the comprehensiveness, originality, and significance of your research.*

Doing original research requires looking where no one else has looked for a solution to your Problem.

Because of the sheer quantity of sources that are searchable online, it is very easy for even the most experienced of researchers to become a kind of passive bystander, allowing the library catalogue or database to demarcate the boundaries of their bibliographies. After all, if you have already "educated your questions," and used the techniques above to discover all of the possible search terms, then what more is there to do than to run all of these keywords through as many databases as possible, and to reap the harvest of thousands of primary sources?

Isn't it time I began searching?

Researchers nowadays often make two major mistakes here. They think that

1. all of the information they need to do their research well is available online; and
2. all of the information available online is searchable.

In fact, digitized materials make up only a small fraction of the total number of primary source materials. The library at Stanford University, where Tom works, is one of the world's most advanced institutions with regard to digitization. Nevertheless, only about 1 percent of Stanford's millions of archival and manuscript materials have been digitized. The rest remain in analog, physical format. Some always will. In limiting ourselves to an online, keyword-driven project, we write off 99 percent or more of potential materials *without even looking at them and perhaps not even knowing that they exist.*

The second mistake researchers make is arguably even more significant. When we allow databases and search results to define the shape and content of our bibliographies, we surrender our critical faculties as researchers. We stop asking critical questions about our subject matter, and we stop using our creativity and our imagination, which would otherwise deepen our engagement with our subject.

Instead of letting keyword searches define the boundaries of your source base, try closing your laptop or your browser, instead *envisioning* in your mind's eye where relevant sources about your subject *might* be located; what these sources *might* look like, in terms of their format and genre; and who or what organization *might* have produced them. In other words, rather than limiting yourself to what *is* (database results), expand your search to include sources that *could be* or even that *must be*.

This is a peculiar exercise in many ways, and one that researchers are typically encouraged not to do. We are not allowed (and for good reason) to "make up" hypothetical sources. In this case, we are asking you to do a slightly different thing.

We believe that this imaginative exercise is one of the things that separates the great researcher from the good one.

Let's say that you are interested in the lives of working-class women in early twentieth-century New York. Rather than running keyword searches, sit back in your chair, stare up at the ceiling (or close your eyes), and ask yourself: Where would the life of a person like this have been recorded? Where might they have left traces of their lives?

Did hospitals in 1920s New York keep records of patients? What kinds of records did schools keep about their students? How about employers? What about immigration documents? Marriage certificates? Baptismal records? Censuses? Criminal cases? Phone books? You could ask the same question about Russian serfs in the 1720s, Austro-Hungarian elites in the 1820s, or Senegalese schoolteachers in the present day.

In a word: What are the archives?

It takes a special form of "education" (see chapter 2) to answer questions like these. You need to know your time and place (New York in 1925 or Trieste in 1825 or Dakar in 2022) well enough to know something about how these societies functioned, and how they produced evidentiary traces. While you may not have any interest in the history of criminal law in the Russian empire or university administration in the United States or customs offices in West Africa—those might not be your primary research "topics" or "problems"—if you know a bit about them, it will help you envision where the people you *are* interested in may have left behind traces of their existence.

Sometimes, in order to get to specifics, you have to think systematically and institutionally.

Think of all the fragments every one of us leaves behind on a weekly, daily, and even hourly and minute-by-minute basis as we go about our days. Credit card payments. Swiping your ID-linked mass transit card on your way to school or work. Yearbook photos. Holiday cards. Traffic tickets. Voter registrations. We leave millions of fragments in a diaspora that spreads across many different domains. Not all can be recovered, of course. Some (we hope) are locked tight in digital vaults. Some will be destroyed before long. Others, even if they were found, could not be linked to you.

Still, some can.

Now imagine someone in the distant future—say, the year 2500—trying to find primary sources through which to reconstruct and understand your life. If that person knew nothing about the history of twenty-first-century credit bureaus, legal systems, voter registration, email, or social media (or did, but ignored them because they decided that those weren't their topic) that researcher would be missing out on troves of materials.

You can see now why you want to take the time to envision sources. Keyword searching is not always the place to start, nor does it turn up all of the results you might need. Instead, you need to envision where sources might exist, and only *then* go back to the work of searching. By then, you will know to look in more and different places. Your list of catalogues, databases, and archives will be larger and more diverse. You'll discover more primary sources, generate more useful questions, and deepen your research in ways you did not anticipate.

The steps for this exercise are straightforward:

1. Write down your research questions, as always, with as much precision as you can.
2. Brainstorm: What sources might exist that would be *primary with respect to* my research questions?
3. Write down as many types of sources as possible.
4. Optional: If you have time to spare, and as long as it doesn't distract you from steps 1 through 3, try to find such sources. If you find any of them, put them through the Cereal Box Challenge.

COMMONLY MADE MISTAKES
- During brainstorming, thinking only in terms of your specific *case* and not in terms of the general categories or institutional structures in which the

> world might have arranged sources related to your case
> - Excluding sources because they do not appear to be related to your topic or keywords
> - Worrying about whether or not you can actually obtain the sources you envision
> - Not writing things down

Connecting the Dots: Getting from Sources to Arguments

Now you have a primary source in front of you, maybe several. Now what? What do I do? How do I make a "thesis-driven argument" out of this source? Where do I begin? What should I take notes about?

All fair questions. And not the only ones.

Your methodological challenges are both practical and ethical:

1. How many primary sources, and which types of primary sources, are enough to do my research?
2. How can I evaluate the reliability or usefulness of sources?
3. How do I identify and exclude irrelevant sources?
4. How do I determine how my sources relate to one another?
5. How do I use various sources to make an argument, or express my degree of certainty or doubt about the argument I am using these sources to make?

That's quite a barrage of questions, so let's take a moment to think about how to connect the dots.

When we're young, many of the puzzles we solve come in a box or in a book. They were created by other people and come to us in the form of prepackaged games: word searches, jigsaw puzzles, anagrams. Someone else already knew the answers, and then crafted a puzzle for us, whether to test our intelligence or to give us fun pastimes.

Remember the game Connect-the-Dots? On the page is a set of dots, each dot accompanied by a number, and the puzzle-solver draws a set of straight lines linking dot 1 to dot 2, dot 2 to 3, and so forth. After connecting all fifty or so dots, the secret image is revealed. In some cases, the image is the answer to a question, like "What is the biggest animal on earth?"

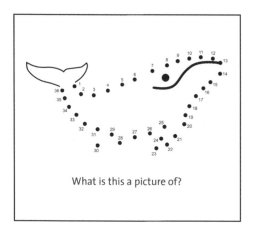

What is this a picture of?

What if, instead of a connect-the-dots puzzle like that, you were presented with one that looked like this:

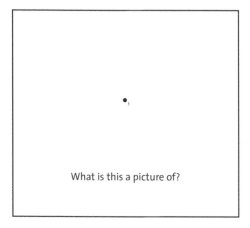

What is this a picture of?

You see the issue here: you can draw an infinite number of lines through a single point (i.e., a single source), and this means that practically any picture — any argument, that is — can be made when based on only one source.

Even with two points, or three, the puzzle is overwhelmingly *unrestricted*.

How do you connect the dots when there's only one dot to connect, or even only a few? How do you begin to chart out interpretations and arguments — the lines of reasoning that connect the dots — when you are just at the very beginning? What if you have only one, two, or three dots to work from? As eager as you may be to make headway in creating "a thesis-driven argument," how can you possibly do so at this stage?

You can't, and you shouldn't try to.

In the early stages of research, faced with an unlimited number of potential questions and interpretations, any attempt to connect the dots rapidly spins out to infinity. The puzzle is unsolvable. An infinite number of lines — for the researcher, narratives and interpretations — can pass through such a small number of "dots," or sources.

Yet the lesson here is not just that you need an adequate number of sources to connect the dots of a good argument. It's more fundamental than that.

Over time, we discover that puzzles no longer come to us prepackaged and ready to solve. To the contrary, the main challenge becomes not solving, but *creating* puzzles that are nontrivial, not preordained, open-ended, and significant (no matter what the answer ends up being). In order to create puzzles, we need to be able to envision and identify unknowns.

Consider, for example, present-day engineering challenges such as self-driving cars or artificial intelligence. These are not fill-in-the-blank or jigsaw-puzzle-style questions. They are questions that are still in the process of being asked in the right way, let alone being solved. *How can we trans-*

form the complexities of human experience into something machine-readable? How do we take such concepts as "life" and "death," and transform them into a stable and comparable set of "life events" that can be captured and digitized? Which types of human behaviors can be predicted, or influenced, using algorithms?

Let's see how we can make the connect-the-dots analogy work for us as researchers. In the opening phases of a new project, the researcher confronts their own kind of connect-the-dots puzzle, but one that behaves differently than either the blue whale or big data examples. Instead of simply taking delivery of a prefabricated, ready-to-solve puzzle, with all the dots present and enumerated, the researcher needs to do the following:

- **Find the dots!** Unlike a puzzle with a predetermined answer, your dots are not all laid out on the page for you, conveniently numbered in sequential order. You might find some dots by chance, but most of them you'll find through purposeful searching.
- **Figure out which dots belong to *your* picture**, and which dots belong to some other picture. Since the dots are not numbered, you need to keep an open mind and be able to envision multiple possible outcomes. An archaeologist who digs in the right place and comes across a deposit of dinosaur bones has the advantage of having all of the bones in one place, but the bones might be mixed with other skeletons, and even if they're not, an archaeologist still needs to figure out which bones attached to which in order to reconstruct the skeleton. A similar issue faces their colleagues excavating ancient Chinese texts from a tomb. Texts were often written on slips of bamboo, which were then tied into order with string. One tomb might include multiple texts. Over centuries underground, the strings disintegrated,

leaving a jumble of bamboo inscriptions. That archaeologist might be lucky enough to have discovered many "dots" in one go, but they still need to distinguish one text from another and then put the bamboo slips in order. Even if you have all of your data points in hand, you still need to know how to analyze them so as to come up with the right solution.

- **Determine which "dots" are *not dots at all*,** but smudges. We call these *non-sources*. Sources are sources because they have utility for the researcher trying to answer a question or solve a problem. Their usefulness is relative — they may be more useful or less. You may recognize an item as being "someone else's" source instead of "your" source, because it's relevant to their Problem. Think of the astronomer trying to discover a new star or galaxy or black hole, who has to filter out the noise of the universe in three dimensions and at great distance. Not everything out there is a source. On the other hand, you might discover that what at first appeared to be a smudge turns out to be something interesting. A single dot could reorient your whole research project.

- **Do all of the above in *real time*.** Not only do the dots not come numbered, and not only do you have to find them, but when you do start finding your dots and making your connections, it is highly unlikely that you will first come across Dot 1, and then Dot 2, and then Dot 3. More likely than not, your first discovery will be Dot 74, followed by Dot 23, and so forth. This places you in the challenging position of having to start interpreting your data without the certainty that you are already in possession of all of it. Visiting another archive, looking at a digital repository, undertaking another day of ethnographic work, another day of an archaeological dig, another day in the chemical compound analysis lab, another oral history interview, or simply another pass at listening to the recording of the interview — these actions add dots to your page. And as more dots appear on your page, the picture becomes clearer. Each additional dot adds a constraint, limiting the number of interpretations that is viable. Where you once had an overwhelming number of possible interpretive lines that could pass through your first few dots, many of those lines disappeared as your data got better. By adding and observing new constraints, you get closer to your answer.

- **Decide when you have enough dots**. Obviously, the answer to the conundrum of how many data points is enough — when to stop digging for bones and when to start writing up the report — will vary by research project. It's during the research process itself that you'll learn to identify thresholds of probability, confidence, and certainty.

Sources Cannot Defend Themselves

Before you connect some dots (not all of them, yet) on your own project, there are ethical issues regarding the use of sources to consider.

One difference between "grown-up" puzzles and the ones we played as children is that *you get to decide how to draw the lines*. In the kiddie puzzles, the lines between two consecutive dots are always drawn straight. The games are designed that way. Writing is a different art form, however, and when you construct the narrative of your arguments and your explanations, or when you tell the story of your research findings, you have the choice of connecting your dots using straight *or* curvy lines — or, most likely, some combination of the two.

Imagine that, in the early phases of our research, we know only five basic facts about a historical person of interest to us:

- date they were born
- city where they grew up
- institution where they pursued their education
- degree they earned
- date they died

Let's consider three very different ways we might connect these dots:

1. The ruler-drawn line (tight; no elaboration)
2. The curved line (loose; some elaboration)
3. The zigzag (extremely loose; highly speculative)

THE RULER-DRAWN LINE

John Smith was born in 1914, and grew up in Chicago. He received a degree in engineering from the University of Illinois. He died in 1989.

This is akin to using a ruler to draw a straight line between our empirical dots, because it "sticks to the facts" and avoids any and all elaboration. At the same time, it could be said to lack interpretive power. It feels static and even lifeless.

Now consider a slightly looser fit.

THE CURVED LINE

John Smith was born in 1914, on the eve of the Great War in Europe. He grew up in Chicago, then a bustling center of industry. He received a degree in engineering from the prestigious University of Illinois. He passed away in 1989.

Here, the researcher's narrative has connected, or "passed through" each of the four dots, and yet they have also supplied additional tone and context to the prose. This supplemental context, although empirically defensible (World War I *did* begin in 1914, and Chicago *was* a center of industry), still represents a choice, even a strategy, by the writer. Was Smith's life *shaped* by the Great War? Was his life *shaped* by the economic history of Chicago? Why or how much does the prestige of the university matter to Smith's life? By "pass away," do they mean he died peacefully? Here the writer is not telling us one way or another in any explicit fashion — they are merely *implying*. As a reader, we wonder: Are these contexts relevant, and defensible?

Now an extremely loose fit.

THE ZIGZAG

John Smith's birth coincided with an event of global historical importance — the outbreak of World War I in 1914 — and his death, yet another — the fall of the Berlin Wall in 1989. He received a degree in engineering from the University of Illinois, a choice shaped perhaps by his upbringing in Chicago, then a bustling center of industry headed by Mayor "Big Bill the Builder" Thompson.

In this third example, the writer is clearly taking undue license. Although they have not uttered any *factually* untrue information — all the dots are accurate, and all of them are connected — a host of dubious cause-and-effect relationships are being implied here, all without a shred of supporting evidence. Was Smith's Chicago upbringing under Thompson's mayoralty the "cause" of him studying engineering? Does it really matter that Smith's birth and death coincided with these events in Europe? (Did the Berlin Wall fall *on* him?) Isn't it the case that one might be able to find major events that coincide with the birth and death years of practically anyone?

A few key takeaways here:

1. **Sources cannot speak for themselves, nor can they defend themselves against you**; thus it is your obligation to represent them accurately. As soon as you start dealing with primary sources, you have to make ethical decisions, the first being to represent the sources as honestly as possible.

2. **Research integrity requires not just dealing in facts but also not forcing them to tell a story.** Fidelity to one's sources is not limited to a question of empirical accuracy. As seen above, even when the author deals entirely in "fact" (the Berlin Wall *did* come down in 1989), there are, nevertheless, ways to connect the dots that "force" them to say things that the author wants them to say.

3. **Connecting the dots from sources to arguments is always a deliberate choice involving ethical responsibility.** Don't be lulled into thinking that your responsibilities as a researcher are satisfied so long as your treatment of sources is "straightforward" or "objective." The "straight-edge" method of connecting the dots is not pure, perfect, or always desirable. A rote inventory of facts can have unwanted effects, such as neglecting essential contexts, or silencing fundamental questions. For a researcher, the connecting of dots *always involves active choice*. The key here is not to avoid or downplay this responsibility, but to make these choices as *deliberately* and *defensibly* as possible. Making decisions is your responsibility as researcher — and at every point, a decision *must* be made.

As you make choices about sources, be aware: even though sources cannot speak for themselves, this does not mean that sources are merely inert objects subject to the will or manipulation of the researcher. They have a kind of agency of their own, even in their seeming silence.

A source might be any of the following:

- Incomplete or fragmentary. In our experience, most sources are.
- Purposefully deceptive — a "pseudo-dot," to use

our earlier terminology. Documents can lie, as can interviewees, objects, and observers.

- Wrong by accident. People (and the various utterances they leave behind — documents, recordings, etc.) can be *unintentionally* deceptive, perhaps because *they* were relying on bad or incomplete information themselves.
- Biased — sincere or well-meaning in trying to tell truth, but distorted by unconscious bias. Maybe at that time they thought the Sun moved around the Earth. Maybe they categorized peoples or plants differently. Maybe they will tell you, because of who they are, "My culture doesn't believe in X." Their claims might be speculative or projecting.
- Motivated by an acknowledged or unacknowledged agenda. They may be trying to persuade you to adopt a certain point of view, or accept a way of thinking.
- Inconsistent. A source might be sometimes reliable and sometimes unreliable. Even the experts make mistakes.

These are just a few reasons why the best researchers adopt a critical, searching mindset. They realize that we always have to question our sources, however reliable or authoritative they may seem. We have to seek corroborating or falsifying evidence, since both are valuable. While evaluating your own sources, use the bullet points above as a checklist, and make a note of further steps you might want to take to understand them better.

Just one more caveat to keep in mind while evaluating sources at this early stage in the research process — and this is a crucial one: even if a source you come across is any of the things described above, *it can still be useful to you, so don't reflexively dismiss it*. Instead, incorporate it into your question-generation process. *Why might this source be trying to deceive me? What phenomenon is this source symptomatic of?* There are no "bad" materials when it comes to generating questions or educating your questions. Radioactive material can be used to generate energy. If you come across a suspect source, use it to generate energy for your own purposes.

TRY THIS NOW:
Connect the Dots Using *Your* Sources (in Pencil)
The goal: *To start thinking about source criticism early in the research process, while remaining flexible and inclusive.*

Does it seem like we're getting ahead of ourselves? After all, you're still gathering sources on your topic and trying to determine their relevance. You are discovering whether or not they are "primary with respect to" your Problem. Isn't it too early to start winnowing them down, or to number the dots and arrange them in a pattern?

Yes, and no.

Research, once again, is a nonlinear process, which is why we keep encouraging you to think through your ideas, your questions, and your sources in a subjunctive mode—to keep thinking *What if?* We want you to take the time to chart and rechart your course as many times as necessary before you launch your journey.

In practical terms, this means being aware of research issues—for example, that you will likely need to *create* your own research puzzle, instead of finding it lying on the ground, ready-made—and trying out different possibilities, without jumping to a question or forcing a project.

For this exercise, try connecting some dots using *your* sources, but do this in pencil so that you can erase the lines and draw new ones later. Assume that you'll have to.

The steps are simple, but they require bringing together some of the work you have done so far on creating self-evidence, and some new thinking about how to synthesize it. Write down answers to these questions, based on wherever you are *right now* in the research process. This is an iterative process, involving repeated corrections and updates, so repeat it as needed later on.

1. Where are my dots (sources)? Draw on what you wrote down for the "Envision Your Primary Sources" exercise.
2. How will I determine which dots belong to my picture, and which to someone else's? Both this and the next question require you to be as honest as possible about the problem that motivates you.
3. How will I determine which of the things I have are actually dots, rather than smudges?
4. What is the best way to arrange my dots, so as to create an accurate, three-dimensional picture? Consider this part of the drafting process: you are trying out some narrative possibilities by structuring and ordering your sources in different configurations, to see how they speak to one another. The key, of course, is not to *force* any pieces of the puzzle together.
5. How many dots will I need to answer my questions, solve my Problem, and complete my project? This is a question that only you can answer, although your Sounding Board might be able to help you make this assessment.

COMMONLY MADE MISTAKES
- Thinking that you have to have *all* your sources in hand before you start this process. You will need to have multiple sources (dots) to begin this process, but not *all*.

- Writing in pen rather than pencil. Recognize that the connections you make between sources right now are necessarily tentative and speculative. Expect that you will have to reassess your judgments later on, and don't think that you have to "stick to" your original thought.

Taking Stock of Your Research Resources

You have some sources. You've started using them to think through your Topic and focus in on your Problem. You've been taking both logistical and ethical factors into consideration, tracking your keyword searches and being mindful of how you are connecting the dots with sources. By now, you should be in a mental space where your ideas are taking shape, even as you remain open-minded about where your research might take you. But to turn research ideas into a research project, you need to take into account an array of other material factors, including the following:

- **Time.** How much time do you realistically have in which to conduct your research? By when do you have to finish the project? Is it possible to do justice to your questions given this amount of time? What other commitments will be competing for your time between now and then?
- **Funding.** How much will it cost for you to carry out the proposed work? What funding is available to you, and what types of research expenses will that funding support? Is it enough? If not, are there ways to relocate your work to make it financially viable, while at the same time preserving your core problem?
- **Writing speed.** Are you the kind of writer who works well on tight deadlines, turning research into text

rapidly? Or does it take you time to mull over your questions? Does your proposed research depend upon an urgent time frame to be of value?

- **Family responsibilities.** How might your relationships affect the time you'll have for research? What types and volume of research will family obligations allow? Are you a caregiver? Will you be able to subdivide your work into shorter segments, spread out over a longer time? Or does the nature of your research require a long, unbroken period of time to complete?

- **Access.** Can you obtain the materials you need to conduct this research? Does your library subscribe to the databases you might need? Will you be able to visit the archives, corporate files, or private papers that you've identified as being essential to the project? Is your proposed research politically sensitive, and if so, do you know whether you will be permitted access to sources?

- **Risk tolerance.** Researchers in war zones, or on volcanoes, place themselves in life-threatening situations. What is your risk tolerance? How about discomfort? Are you capable of working over long periods of time away from, say, access to medical facilities, electricity, and running water? Be realistic.

- **Abilities.** What is your skill set, or that of your research team? What languages do you speak and read? Do you have the necessary expertise to conduct this research?

- **Human subjects.** Does your proposed research include work with at-risk populations (such as marginalized communities or children)? Do you need ethics board approval for research involving human subjects? Have you prepared adequately and rigorously to handle the particular challenges of such research, in terms of confidentiality, data security, and more? Can you keep your sources safe, or would your work endanger them?

- **Personality.** One of the most abstract, yet also most important, factors to consider is your own personality. While the binary of "extrovert" and "introvert" is a blunt tool with which to categorize sensibilities, ask these key questions: In which kinds of situations do I find my internal battery recharged, and in which situations is it drained? Do frequent social interactions leave me feeling energized, or do I prefer solitary work? With this in mind, what kind of research will my work realistically entail? Will it entail long hours of solitary reading? Or will it involve morning-to-night lab work or fieldwork, where time to myself will be scarce or nonexistent?

The point here is not to be "essentialist" about yourself, your identity, and your capacities. No matter who you think yourself to be right now, remember that research is a powerful process that can and often does challenge and even *transform* the researcher. So don't be surprised if it brings out aspects of your character that you didn't know existed. Likewise, in some cases a project might feel so important to a researcher — their sense of commitment may be so strong — that just this once they are willing to work beyond their comfort zone.

Just remember: it is OK to recognize your own limits and to act in accordance with them. It is equally OK *not* to pursue a project that would cause you harm.

And above all, know this: even in those cases when you decide not to pursue a project, this is not tantamount to abandoning yourself or your underlying problem. As we have hinted at earlier, and as we explore in more depth later in this chapter, it is possible to find your Problem in another project, and to pursue it just as meaningfully and just as rigorously.

TRY THIS NOW: Decision Matrix

The goal: *To envision which factors will likely have the greatest impact, positive or negative, on the success of your research project, and to adjust your plan accordingly.*

TABLE 6. MATERIAL FACTORS

• Time	• Family responsibilities	• Abilities
• Funding	• Access	• Human subjects
• Writing speed	• Risk tolerance	• Personality

Table 6 lists several material factors.

Using table 7 as your guide, follow these steps:

1. Create an inventory of all of the factors that could impact the success of your project as you currently imagine it. Aim for a list of ten to fifteen factors. You might phrase them as follows:

    "I like talking to strangers." (personality)

    "I have to do daycare pickup at 3pm, M-F." (family responsibilities)

    "I'm great at math, and I love statistics." (abilities)

    "I will only be able to do field research if I get grant X." (funding)

2. Categorize each factor as positive or negative. For example, if you thrive in social settings, and draw energy from meeting and interacting with complete strangers, you could categorize this as a positive factor, if you envision a project involving extensive interviewing. By contrast, if you grapple with severe anxiety in social settings, then this might count as a negative factor.

3. Categorize each factor as high-, medium-, or low-impact, depending on the degree to which you believe it will affect your project.

Something to keep in mind about step 2: when we speak of "positive" and "negative" factors, the goal is not to cast judgments about ourselves as people—there is nothing fundamentally better or worse about being an extrovert or an introvert—but rather to assess the compatibility between the project you envision and yourself as a human being. The goal is to take an inventory that will give you an honest, unvarnished overview of the different factors that will shape your project.

TABLE 7. CREATE A DECISION MATRIX

HIGH-IMPACT	Factor 1	Factor 2	Factor 3	Factor 4
Positive				
Negative				
MEDIUM-IMPACT	Factor 1	Factor 2	Factor 3	Factor 4
Positive				
Negative				
LOW-IMPACT	Factor 1	Factor 2	Factor 3	Factor 4
Positive				
Negative				

Feel free to add other factors and to add more columns to your own table, as necessary.

Create an outline, or list if/then scenarios for these factors, if that helps you.

Whichever approach you choose, while mapping out what it might take to carry out your project, include as much detail as possible and be honest with yourself about your own capacities and limitations. Indicate clearly which factors will be the most decisive and which will be the least decisive. Use this hierarchy to figure out your probabilities of success with different types of research projects. Adjust your research questions accordingly.

COMMONLY MADE MISTAKES
- Underestimating the amount of time it will take to complete the project
- Listing only "professional" factors and failing to include personal factors that might have a real effect on your research progress
- Neglecting to consider ethical factors such as the effects of human-subject research on participants

SOUNDING BOARD:
Is Your Decision Matrix Complete?
After you've done your own assessment of the practicalities of various research scenarios and written them down in your decision matrix, discuss them with your Sounding Board. They might be able to point out sources or research tools (or constraints) you weren't aware of, or to introduce you to people with firsthand experience of the archive you hope to visit. A conversation with your mentor can be an efficient way to refine your scope.

Two Types of Plan B

We hope that everything works out well for you, of course, and that your intended research proceeds smoothly. In case it doesn't, however, you want to be ready to pursue other possible pathways. As researchers, much of what we do is a plan B of one kind or another. Best to learn early on that being flexible is part of the job description. One of the thrills of research, in fact, is overcoming a challenge or being nimble enough to bypass a roadblock to accomplishing your goal.

Consider these two scenarios.

SCENARIO 1: SAME PROBLEM, DIFFERENT CASE

What do you do when you've found the right *problem*, but the *project* you envision cannot be done for practical reasons?

A student in Tom's History of Information class came to office hours to discuss a paper topic. The student was interested in activism and protest and the relationship between social media–based online organization and real-world offline organization. How did the two relate, if at all? Black Lives Matter (BLM) was of particular concern to the student, and so their question as originally formulated was, How have BLM activists used online organization techniques in support of real-world demonstrations and actions?

The topic and question were great, but the methodological obstacles were daunting: if the student had months to interview BLM activists, engage in ethnographic research, and gain trust and access to personal accounts and records of their activities (texts, emails, etc.), this could be a stellar project. But the student had mere weeks to formulate and complete the project, no way to access private collections, nor time to engage in the ethnographic fieldwork necessary to form a credible empirical basis. The student had a great set of questions, but the conditions were just not in place for the project to succeed as envisioned. Not even a seasoned researcher could complete such a project in a few weeks without doing serious injustice to the complexities of the subject matter.

What to do?

Instead of abandoning the problem, the student and Tom carried on the conversation, trying to get at the deeper layers of the question. Instead of getting overly distracted by terms like "social media" and "online organization," they tried to identify the underlying stakes involved — what each of these terms was a "case of." Was the student's interest fundamentally connected to Twitter and Facebook? (*No, not necessarily.*) Would other kinds of telecommunications and information technologies also be of interest — say, technologies like the telephone, or even the telegraph, if we were to imagine a BLM movement happening in, say, the 1910s or the 1960s? (*Yes.*)

What about earlier civil rights movements? Did the focus have to be Black Lives Matter or would something from further back in history be valid as well? (*Yes, but it would have to be a movement that addressed racial inequalities in particular.*)

These exercises enabled the student to identify the underlying "problem" of their questions remarkably quickly.

Suddenly, the researcher had opened up a world of possible cases to consider, all while keeping their core problem constant. *How did the Freedom Riders or Martin Luther King Jr. or the Student Nonviolent Coordinating Committee (SNCC) use communication technologies in the course of their operations? Or, perhaps, how did Gandhi or Cesar Chavez? In particular, how did these organizations use technology, not simply to organize marches well in advance, but in the course of "real-time" emergencies: the arrest of key members, the need to respond to physical emergencies, the need to communicate to news media outlets in the context of constantly changing circumstances — operations that we now take for granted in the internet age?*

Suddenly, carrying out this research project no longer depended upon having years and years to do ethnographic research, or gaining access to the private diaries of political activists. Because the student was aware of the problem underlying their work, it was going to be possible to pursue that problem by different means. The chances of finding a relevant body of primary sources became significantly higher, whether in analog format (in the archives at a nearby library, museum, or college) or via online archives.

The key point here is that when you as a researcher know what is *core* to your research problem, rather than what is merely a "case" of it, this gives you a kind of passport with which you can travel to all kinds of different places, times, and communities — all without leaving behind your research "center." What is more, even if this student had, right after this conversation with Tom, happened upon a previously unknown repository of primary source materials connected to Black Lives Matter — something that could be explored in time for a final project — this introspective process would still enable the student to approach this case with the insight that only comes with knowing what the core stakes are in the research question. Rather than, for example, assuming that BLM's techniques of organization are fundamentally unprecedented, all thanks to the existence of social media, the student would be able to situate this "online-offline" dyad within a broader historical context of, say, technologically mediated communication and on-the-ground organization. Either way, the student's research would enrich their understanding of the problem.

In short, being realistic does not mean abandoning your ideals. Blue-sky thinking can sometimes lead to viable research projects. But if your ambitions outstrip your resources, don't give up hope. Simply return to the problem that underlies your questions and your project, and seek out another case that might let you pursue it.

SCENARIO 2: SAME TOPIC, DIFFERENT PROJECT
What do you do when the project you envision could theoretically be done, *just not by you*?

As we saw in the Black Lives Matter example, knowing their core Problem enables a researcher to locate it in any number of different cases. You might have thought that you were exclusively concerned with Brazil or women's literature, but then, by way of discovering your actual Problem, you realized that both "Brazil" and "women's literature" were in fact cases of that Problem. And this now frees you to relocate your project in different ways.

But there are other limits to the cases you could choose that go beyond questions of the ability of sources or time limits. Choosing the right case for your Problem is also a question of temperament. It needs to fit who you are as a person. Let's say you want to understand the interior lives of communities who live in the margins of contemporary society: individuals living in homeless encampments in your city, unemployed youth in the Rust Belt, individuals struggling with mental health challenges, or undocumented migrants. As marginalized communities, they may not have the power to shape the narratives the rest of the world uses to understand them — and this disturbs you, emotionally and intellectually.

But let's also say that you are a deeply introverted person, one who experiences social anxiety. Are you prepared to carry out a project that will likely require you to engage in extensive fieldwork over long stretches of time? Are you able to sustain yourself in contexts where you are perhaps far from your own loved ones, from your own routines, from your support systems for extended periods of time? Are you able to take care of yourself in the context of immersion of this kind?

If the answer is "yes," then perhaps this is the case for you. If the answer is "maybe not," *don't feel bad about it.* And, even more importantly, *don't try to deny it.* You may worry that, if you give up on your case, then you have to give up on your Problem as well — but this isn't so. As long as you are in tune with your Problem, and truly understand what it is, then it is possible to change your case quite dramatically *without abandoning the underlying problem that excites and disturbs you.* If you're not sure how to do that, begin again with more introspective work to help you understand your underlying problem. More insight about your *motivations* will in turn make finding another compelling and appropriate case much easier.

Now that we've examined some of the common ways a project can be thrown off course, as well as how best to pivot, let's consider some of the more nuts-and-bolts tasks that go into designing a project that works: setting up your workspace, choosing the right tools, and planning a work schedule tuned to your needs.

Setting Up Shop

Research is a craft. And as a craftsperson, it's important that you set up your shop just the way you like it. If you have friends who are serious artists or musicians, you know how much they love to talk about their instruments, tools, and work habits. Painters search for the perfect brushes, violinists for the perfect bows, oboists for the perfect reeds, and guitarists for the perfect strings. The same is true for chefs and their knives; fishermen and their lures; mechanics and their machines.

You'll thank yourself if you take the time to think through the design of your work environment. You'll be spending a lot of time in this physical space and using these tools. Remember how we said in chapter 1 that with questions it's best to start small? When setting up shop, details matter too. Get a few seemingly minor things right and you'll reap the gains in increased motivation, productivity, and happiness. There is nothing superficial about giving due attention to physical conditions, since it will affect the well-being of you and your research.

Assess which research tools are worth investing in, given your available resources and what you want to accomplish. Will you be doing a lot of interviewing? You'll need a microphone, a recorder, and a storage and retrieval system. Will you be composing voice notes in the field? You might want to invest in reliable voice-to-text software, and a long-lasting battery. Concert pianists might shell out more money for a piano than the rest of us would (or could) for a car because for them it's not a luxury. A well-funded researcher might be able to accomplish more by hiring assistants, but this is not an option for all of us. Consider what you need (wants are secondary), so that you can set up shop in a way that is "perfect for me, here and now."

When a paring knife or a calligraphy brush sits in one's hand just right, it makes the act of preparing a meal or composing a work of art incrementally more joyous, inviting, and sometimes seemingly effortless. The same is true for you as a researcher, and so you should give thought to your tools and your workspace.

Here are some of the things you will need for your shop to run smoothly.

THE RIGHT TOOLS

If you write by hand, your choice of pen or pencil matters. Does the graphite in your pencil have the right texture for you? Does it dull or break too often? Do your pen and your writing surface have a nice bite, or does the ink spill out messily (and does that bother you)? How quickly does your hand grow fatigued? Likewise, do you need a $25 leather-bound blank book to get you in the writing mood, or will a $2 cellophane-wrapped sheaf of loose-leaf paper from the local drugstore do the trick? Even this type of decision can have real consequences. The blank book might inspire you to take writing more seriously, and thus to invest more energy in it. Maybe it "slows you down" in a good way, inspiring you to take more time to think through your ideas. A bound book, in contrast, can be intimidating, its price tag and design almost scoffing at you as you lift your pen. *This had better be good*, you can almost hear it say. You convince yourself that passing thoughts are unworthy of the journal, and try to save its pristine pages for those moments when you truly have something "worthwhile" to say. Every thought must be complete, every sentence sparkling. Drafts and fragmentary thoughts must never besmirch its pages. Your paper choice has led to disaster. Writing and note-taking are hard enough on their own. None of us needs an added inhibition. Perhaps you'd benefit from a less reverent relationship with your writing surface.

These might all seem like inconsequential things, but everything about your workspace will shape your desire to write, the rate at which you will lose steam, and even the quality and tone of your prose. If you use a note-taking system that subconsciously makes you feel rushed and bottled up, like a tiny memo pad, *this will affect your work*. Your ideas will have less space to unfold, and you'll constantly be cutting yourself short. By the same token, a note-taking system that feels cumbersome and inconvenient (like an app that requires you to have Wi-Fi access at all times, or a large sketch pad, which is hard to transport) can easily result in writing less often. Like other artists, musicians, and craftspersons, you have every right to be choosy about your tools.

THE RIGHT TIME OF DAY

When to write? More specifically, at *what time of day* should you focus on *what type of writing*? The answer varies widely from person to person, but here is a rule of thumb: do the "heavy lifting" when you're fresh and focused, and the more "mindless" work when you're tired or distracted. If you're most alert in the morning, or late at night, then that is when you should write new prose. By contrast, many of us experience fatigue or distraction at other times of day. These are good times to pivot and work on those forms of writing that demand less creative engagement: cleaning up footnotes, spell-checking, and the like.

Writing also has its seasons, and sometimes you have to

let the project lie fallow to let the soil regenerate. Take a break and go for a walk. Watch a movie. Exercise. Have a meal. Sleep. You may feel like you are taking "time away" from your work — and, indeed, you are. But the truth is, chances are your mind is still at work on the puzzle of writing, and may even untie some complex knots without any conscious effort on your part at all. When this happens (and it happens often!) a writer returns to the page and can sometimes feel as if someone else must have solved the problem or cracked the code for them — because suddenly something that seemed overwhelmingly complex or difficult to articulate simply flows, effortlessly.

You can also ask someone, or *something*, to read your work to you. When you simply cannot bear the thought of reading through your draft another time, ask a friend to narrate it aloud. Or, if that's simply too much to ask of even a close friend, use one of the readily available "text-to-audio" functions that translates written text into spoken audio. Sit back, or stand up, and simply *listen* to your draft, narrated to you in sometimes comically awkward computerized voices. What you will discover is that even when you are unable to detect typos in your draft, having become too familiar with the text to spot them anymore, you will somehow be able to "spot" them immediately when you listen. Something will simply feel "off," prompting you to return to the text, locate the culprit, and fix the error.

Listen for cadence as well. Is the prose lyrical and patient, or does it feel rushed in parts? Are there any stretches of self-indulgent prose? Are there any points you are belaboring, or perhaps long stretches in need of a segue? Or maybe one paragraph has too many sentences all of the same length, and the passage is crying out for variation.

Remember that when someone does read your work, they don't just download it instantly into their minds. Reading is an *experience*, and it's up to you to make that experience a fulfilling one.

Get Money for Nothing (Prepare a Formal Research Proposal)

The goal: *To catalyze all of the "potential energy" you've been building up thus far, by giving it a sudden, unexpected jolt—namely, by writing a formal, forward-looking prospectus about your project-in-the-making, where you try to persuade someone to support your work. This research prospectus will also bring into even sharper focus your assumptions* right now *about what other people might find compelling about your study. This is* definitely *going to feel premature, but trust us: it's still part of the process.*

Up till now, we've been urging you to focus on introspection, and to avoid worrying about the outside world. We've urged you to identify and trust your own instincts. Even while looking at search results and examining primary sources, your goal has been to think of your project from the inside out, not the outside in.

For this exercise, however—just for a moment—you're going to become an extrovert. You're going to take the self-dialogue you've been having and turn it outward, explaining your project to an imaginary reader in as coherent and persuasive a manner as you can at this point. And you're going to do it all *before* you're ready.

What is the title of your research project?

What are your main research questions?

Why have other people failed to ask those questions, or to answer them well?

What are the primary sources you need in order to answer your questions and address your Problem?

A word of caution (but also comfort): you are *not* going to feel ready for this. In fact, you *shouldn't*. After all, how could you possibly know how to explain the point of a project that is still in formation? But there's no time to fret about this. Imagine that it's the morning of a big exam, or a job interview, only that late the night before a power outage reset your alarm or let your smartphone battery run out. Your eyes open, and the realization hits you like a wave: *I've got to go!*

Don't have a title? *Make one up!* Don't have a final list of primary sources you'll need? *Finalize it!* Haven't finished thinking through the potential implications of your work? *Open your mouth and start talking. The curtain is up, you're on stage, and the audience is waiting.* In short, pretend for a moment that you are much further along in the research process than you actually are, and try to convince a research-funding agency to choose your project over all of the many other deserving applications it receives every year.

Why in the world would we recommend such a thing? Isn't the whole point of this book *introspection, patience, centeredness*? Yes, but keep in mind two important things.

First, research requires imagination. Yes, research requires other qualities, like competence, tenacity, and honesty. You have to do a ton of note-taking, along with meticulous record-keeping, fact-checking, and source citation. But research is not merely transcription or stenography or the precise replication of existing ideas. Research depends on one's ability to envision realities and ideas that *don't yet exist.* And because they don't exist yet, *no amount of preparation will ever leave you "100 percent ready" to begin.*

Simply put, you *never* know enough to begin.

The adage applies as much to someone who has years to complete their project as to someone who has only weeks. And yet: if you don't begin, you'll never finish.

Counterintuitive as it might seem, then . . .

Before you write a single page of your book, give it a title.

Before you shoot a single frame of your documentary, give it a name.

Go even further. Write a *review* of the book you've yet to write. Write a blurb for the dust jacket. Now write a scathing review. Now write your *rebuttal*.

Remember when we spoke of the "*executive* part of you that speaks, but does not know," and the "*intuitive* part of you that knows, but cannot speak"? Up to now, we've been focusing on building up the intuitive side. As we saw with that student of feng shui, if you *ignore* or *suppress* intuition, you might never get started, or you might end up executing the wrong plan. But if you *listen* to your intuition first, the executive side's job is much easier. The insights come pouring out.

Now is the time to let that "executive" part of you back in the room, since now you know what it needs to do. Instead of shouting down your intuitive side, or trampling over it with big words, that executive part of you will now be working *in collaboration with and in service of* your intuitive part.

And something magical will happen. At first, maybe you'll cringe every time you write a definitive-sounding sentence—because, deep down, you'll know just how undefined everything still is. Your air of certainty will seem forced. You might even feel like a fraud.

But, then . . . you'll write a sentence, and maybe another, that makes you stop and think: *Wait. That's not too bad.* Not every sentence is a keeper, but these sentences are good. You'll read over what you wrote and realize: *I never thought of that before. This is a new idea. I might be onto something!* It's a strange feeling, as if the words were written by someone else.

What is happening is this: under the stress of having to articulate ideas that are still inchoate and underdeveloped, your executive intelligence will kick into auto-pilot and start to assemble one "smart-sounding" sentence after the next. It will iron out the wrinkles, and fill in the gaps and crevices, building up paragraphs that—to the undiscerning eye—actually seem like the author knows what they're talking about.

The second thing to keep in mind is this: this exercise is *still* part of the introspective process. It's still taking place "behind closed doors." You shouldn't *really* submit this proposal to public scrutiny. The reason to do this type of envisioning now—even before you have done all of the due diligence on what other research exists on your topic—is to produce a type of self-evidence that you can generate *only* in this raw, unpolished state. Every time you delay your "start date," telling yourself, *Just one more source!* another one of your rough edges will be sanded down and smoothed out, your fresh, exploratory mindset slowing giving way to something more formal and "professional."

The polish will come later. For now, what you need most of all is to articulate, in written form, *your* earliest thoughts on a subject. *Your* agenda.

What were my initial thoughts, back when I was still in that fresh, exploratory mindset? I never wrote them down, because I assumed I wasn't ready to start. This is one lamentation you never want to have as a researcher.

Completing this exercise will not only create a record of those thoughts, but will help firm up your self-centered foundation, preparing you for the next big step you'll take in part 2 of delving into the wider world of scholarship.

So, try this.

Prepare a research grant proposal in which you articulate a research question and argue that someone should give you money to answer it. Force yourself to be clear and concise by writing a formal document, within tight constraints:

- 4–6 double-spaced pages
- 1-inch margins
- Times New Roman, 12-point font
- Due in one week (to be submitted to yourself only!)

Make your case with confidence. No need to reveal just how tentative many of your ideas still are. It's time to ask your questions out loud, and to proclaim your Problem clearly. Be bold, even if it all feels a bit premature.

The research proposal should contain the following four parts. (Sample proposals to help you jumpstart the process can be found at whereresearchbegins.com.)

1. **Contextual framework.** Briefly situate your reader in time and space. Pretend you are writing a paper for a faceless committee of reviewers whom you have never met, and who may not have the same level of expertise with your subject matter. You need to equip them by explaining (succinctly but thoroughly) the essential knowledge and frames of reference that they will need to understand the facts of your proposed research and appreciate its potential significance.

2. **Goals and objectives.** State the questions you propose to answer using primary source archival materials. It is OK, even essential, for you to include more than one question, so long as they collectively "add up" to a meaningful and coherent constellation of questions that helps you explore a specific, researchable, and meaningful question. This is a proposal for funding/future research, and

so you are encouraged to frame your project as exploratory research with open-ended questions. At the same time, this section should prepare your reader for the case you will be making in part 2 about the potential significance of your findings.

3. **Significance.** Based on your current understanding of your chosen area of analysis, explain the significance of your proposed questions. Why, given what we already know about your topic, would our understanding be significantly improved by your project? And remember: since this is a proposal for future research, rather than completed research, you cannot justify "significance" based on any "hoped-for outcome." That is to say, the significance of your proposed questions cannot be pegged to one expected answer to such questions, otherwise your research will likely lead to foregone conclusions. Rather, the significance of your proposal must reside in a well-articulated, meaningful, and *open-ended* problem that you have arrived at through primary source–based (and secondary source–based) research.

4. **Project plan.** Which specific primary sources would you plan to use to undertake this project, and where are they located? Additionally, if your project were approved, and you received travel funds, which fieldwork site would you visit, interviews would you conduct, datasets would you access, archival collections would you use, etc.? (Be as specific as possible here. For example, cite interviewees and/or archival collections by name, if possible.) Provide a detailed methodology that will enable you to achieve your project goals. What texts, observations, or other source materials will

you need to answer your question? What analytical framework will you use to understand or interpret these sources? Provide a logistical plan, including your timeline and list of project milestones.

COMMONLY MADE MISTAKES
- Avoiding writing this draft by using one of the oldest procrastination tricks in the book: "I just need to do a little bit more research." Save that for later. For now, however, think and write from where you are *at this moment.*
- Writing defensively. Anticipate things that your reader might ask about or challenge, certainly, but do so in the service of drawing attention to the potential contributions of your project. Don't tell us what we *won't* learn, but what we *will.* This is the time for positive thinking.
- Adopting a tentative, unsure, or apologetic tone. When you are envisioning your ideal research-future, do so with confidence. Say "I will . . ." instead of "I will attempt to . . ."

SOUNDING BOARD: Share Your Proposal with a Trusted Mentor (Who Understands How Preliminary This Is)

Read through your own proposal. Is it persuasive? What questions might someone ask about your goals, sources, methods, assumptions? Anticipate these questions and revise your document accordingly. Then—and this is totally optional—show it to someone you trust and solicit their feedback. Explain the goal of this drafting exercise, as described above. Does the proposal make an effective case for why this project is compelling and important? If your mentor didn't know that this was *your* proposal, would they give the applicant the money? Why or why not? Which parts of the proposal do they think could be improved? Oral or written feedback are both welcome, but if possible set up an in-person meeting to hear what they have to say. Write down their suggestions, and then—be sure to do this before proceeding to part 2—*rewrite your proposal based on the suggestions you agree with.*

Then send a message of thanks.

You Have the Beginnings of a Project

Everything is now in place. You've checked and clarified your own motivations and interests. You've settled on research questions and identified the underlying problem that these questions belong to. You've identified the assumptions that brought you here, and you've taken ownership of them.

If you still harbor some doubts, take note of them. Write them down. But remember that you are still drafting. Uncertainties are normal. Everything, in fact, is provisional until the study is complete, and a researcher should always remain open-minded and ready to change as facts warrant. If, at this stage, you feel grave misgivings about the direction things are going, you can revisit the exercises you found most useful, and double-check to make sure that you have avoided the commonly made mistakes. But don't worry. In part 2, you will find even more useful techniques for articulating, evaluating, testing, and rethinking your Problem. You're not done with introspection.

For now, take another moment to review what you've done. By this point, you should have a good sense of what the stakes of this research are for you, and why the results will be meaningful. You've also taken some pragmatic steps:

doing an initial review of some primary sources, taking stock of your abilities and constraints, seeking advice from your Sounding Board when necessary, and choosing the type of project that best suits your temperament. You've even written out a first-draft research proposal, envisioning your project in formal terms. And you've been writing all along.

Now it's time to begin your project.

Part 2

. . . .

Get Over Yourself

In moving from topic to questions, from questions to a problem, and from a problem to the beginnings of a project—still an embryonic one—you've been building a research agenda and a plan. You've made your assumptions visible. You've identified the stakes involved in your research problem. You've also done reality checks, assessing if your project is right for you as a whole person, not just a brain in a box. And all the while, you haven't just been plotting things out in your mind; you've been writing all along and are well on your way to developing your research project. You may well have finished the hardest part.

Your project matters to you. Does it matter to the world?

Answering that question is part of your next major challenge: *getting over yourself.*

You've worked hard at delving into yourself—getting to know the questions and problems that propel your work forward, and taking stock of your preconceptions, abilities, and constraints. But now you need to venture *beyond* yourself and to translate all of these questions and problems in ways that will allow others to understand them. If you do your work well, "your Problem" will become "*their* Problem," too. Part 2 shares some techniques for doing so. If you follow them closely, other people will become as disturbed by your questions as you are — they will make your passion *their* passion.

You might well wonder: *Why did I spend so much time delving into myself if I'm just going to have to "get over" myself? Now that I've finally found my calling, why would you ask me to abandon it?*

The answer is, You're not abandoning anything. "Getting over yourself" does not mean turning your back on all the insights you generated through introspection. Far from it. You'll be continuing that introspective work, but now in relation to other people's ideas too. Getting over yourself is a movement from a more narrow understanding of self to a more expansive one.

This process of exploration, discovery, and accretion is based on engagement. You learn new vocabularies and grammars. You also find common grammars, even when the vocabulary is different. Far from *losing* your sense of self, seeing your ideas in relation to others' can help you to *learn even more* about yourself. After all, you can learn a second or third language without forgetting your mother tongue.

Another reason to get over yourself is entirely pragmatic: none of us, even when we do much of our work alone, inhabit a research community of one. Whether we realize it or not, when we launch a research project, we are joining multiple, ongoing conversations, some defined by a shared interest in a particular type of problem, others defined by the approach to solving the problem or by its intersection with a particular area of knowledge. In the creation of any new research, we rely on the ideas of predecessors and peers.

One of the most important conversations you'll be joining is with the broader community of researchers who work on the same topic as you — a community commonly referred to as a "field." Chris, for example, did a PhD in the field of literature — specifically, modern Chinese literature — and he later expanded his research and teaching into cinema studies. Tom's field is history — the history of modern China and the history of technology. In chapter 5, we discuss ways to navigate your Field, and to rethink the concept of field itself. But this book would never have been written if we hadn't ventured outside our respective fields.

The other conversation you'll be joining — and this requires the bigger shift in thinking about how we do research — is with a community of researchers who work on the same *problem* as you. As it is the problem and not the topic that is at the center of the Self-Centered Research method, part 2 begins by introducing, in chapter 4, the concept of the Problem Collective.

The overarching goal for part 2 is to become aware of how other people's agendas and questions intersect with our own, and to make the most of those relationships. Research is never a monologue, and your research identity is not static. You have to navigate your Field (and might change or add Fields), which involves interacting with different Problem Collectives. Doing so requires remaining mobile and open-minded. Yet the key to engaging with the ideas of others is to maintain your own sense of centeredness.

Part 2 moves your research journey into a broader and deeper engagement with other people's ideas. You'll be on the hunt for compelling, critical, and relevant thinkers. Once again, you'll be stress-testing your ideas, assumptions, and theories, but this time you'll be doing so using the ideas, assumptions, and theories of others. You will make other people's ideas your own. Eventually, you'll help other people make *your* ideas *their* own.

All of this requires being receptive to change. You'll be engaged in a balancing act of seeking out best practices, common goals, new data and insights without losing confidence in the face of established authorities or letting others supplant your agenda with their own. You'll be adopting a dis-position that is self-confident and self-aware, but also open to and curious about what other people have to say. The pro-cess can be exhilarating.

Get ready to get over yourself.

4. How to Find Your Problem Collective

• •

Identify Researchers Who Share Your Problem

You are not the only person who cares about your Problem. It disturbs other people too. Some, driven by the same existential irritant as you, are busy at this very moment asking their own questions, gathering their own sources, identifying their own cases, and formulating their own projects. They might call themselves historians, philosophers, archaeologists, economists, anthropologists, performance studies scholars, classicists, literary scholars, artists. They might work on the 1800s or the ancient world. They may live in Bogota or Baltimore or Beirut.

Some are already dead. What you call *your* Problem was *their* Problem long before. And you have something to learn from them. Those who are still alive, or have yet to be born, have something to learn from you. Whoever they are, wherever they are, you need to find them. But how?

If libraries or bookstores were organized according to problems, rather than topics, their shelves would not be labeled "Current Affairs," "Children's Books," "History," and the like. Each section would be named after the underlying problem shared by a set of authors, regardless of genre.

Imagine walking through the door:

> YOU: Pardon me. Where is your section on *authors-who-wonder-if-authentic-self-expression-is-possible-in-a-*

world-permeated-by-institutions-that-seek-financial-gain-by-selling-us-the-fiction-that-self-expression-requires-the-consumption-of-their-products?

BOOKSTORE CLERK: It's in the back-left aisle, right next to *authors-who-wonder-if-the-seemingly-universal-concept-of-deception-can-be-examined-through-culturally-specific-interpretive-matrices-rather-than-subordinated-to-Eurocentric-ones.*

YOU: Thanks!

As we all know, this is not how bookstores are organized. Nor libraries, university departments, government agencies, corporations, or museums . . . You've just spent considerable effort moving away from topics and toward questions and problems, only to arrive at a disquieting truth: the world at large is organized according to—you guessed it—*topics*. Dreadful as it may sound, you now find yourself back in the vague and all-too-familiar world where you started.

You are back in Topic Land.

What to do? By now you have a strong sense of what disturbs you, and yet the mainstream organizational logic of everything around you returns you to those overarching "topics" that bear no direct connection to problems. Within our topic-centric world, how to find the community of researchers who share your Problem? How do you find your *Problem Collective*?

Problem Collective is a concept for envisioning the various problem-centric intellectual connections and affiliations we can discover and create during the research process.

A collective is a grouping of individuals who share an interest or enterprise. A Problem Collective is—you guessed it—a grouping of individuals working to solve the same research problem whether together or independently. You could call it a gang, a tribe, or a community—the metaphor isn't important. What matters is the appreciation that this group is comprised of *individuals*, each with their own personal "center," and that its membership is dispersed and decentralized — so much so that members may well be unaware of one another's existence. This collective is not an ideological faction bound by shared dogma. It is not a militia or a cult.

Problem Collective is not another name for a profession, a department, a field, or a discipline. Fields like history or political science *contain* members of various Problem Collectives (as we'll discuss in chapter 5), but they are not Problem Collectives themselves. While members of fields and disciplines share many things in common, fields and disciplines themselves are not defined by a commonly held problem. One great virtue of finding your Problem Collective is that it can free you from disciplinary silos, professional identities, and the reflexive conservatism that convinces you that your research agenda must fall within the boundaries of your Field.

A Problem Collective is a community whose members — whatever their background, field, or discipline — find themselves compelled by a common, profound problem. This problem typically cannot be reduced to anything exclusive to a single time period or place. Someone concerned with a problem related to loss or freedom or equality or meaning could work on any number of cases of that problem. They might just as readily write a work of philosophy or a children's pop-up book. Problems — especially those that tap into universal themes — can trouble people from all dispositions, worldviews, politics, and walks of life.

A Problem Collective might be small or large. It includes members of your Field — including you, of course — and members of potentially many other fields too. (We'll say more about fields in the next chapter.) Given that members of your Problem Collective can be dispersed widely, and given that they rarely wear identifying badges, finding them can feel daunting. This chapter offers you several strategies for doing so.

But why take the effort to find such a collective? Why not just work solo? Or why not just stick to your Field?

When you find your Problem Collective, it gives you

- questions you'd never considered before,
- a vocabulary you were unaware of,
- perspectives and vantage points you did not know existed,
- techniques you never knew about, and
- a sense of validation and community.

A Problem Collective reminds you that it is OK to worry intensively about the problem that, until now, you perhaps thought was unique to you.

More than this, even, finding your collective empowers you and gives you license to pursue a line of inquiry that is not bound by field or discipline. By bringing you into communion with researchers, present and past, living and dead, all grappling with your same concerns, it reminds you that you have every right to engage with the works of luminary thinkers. You can speak with whomever was or is preoccupied with the same concerns as you.

A Problem Collective also challenges you, revealing that the true purpose of studying such figures is not merely to do well on your final exam, to appear learned, or to expand your mind in some vague kind of way, but rather because maybe, just maybe, one of these thinkers holds part of the key to *solving your Problem*.

Suddenly, you have no reason to be intimidated by famous, brand-name thinkers. You also become immune to the prejudices of people who dismiss concerns about theory and methodology as "academic," in the pejorative sense — the same people who talk about the "life of the mind" as if it were detached from "real life." You can now reject such artificial distinctions, because you know that a problem, and the quest to solve it, are as much a part of real life as you are.

But let's be honest about this: it can take time to grasp

the problem that underlies your many questions, and then to find members of your Problem Collective. Months sometimes, even years. And it's easy to lose oneself in "the literature," in all of the good ideas and compelling agendas already out there. The techniques introduced in this chapter will enable you to cleave to your Problem, even as you spend more time engaging with the works of other researchers.

In order to find members of your Problem Collective, you first need to confront one of research's most challenging puzzles: *What does the world call* my *Problem?*

TRY THIS NOW: Change One Variable

The goals: *To distinguish between the problem and a* case *of the problem. To identify which components of a research question are "indispensable" to that question, and are thus most indicative of the underlying research problem you are trying to solve. You will then be better able to identify other studies that share your Problem.*

Is there a way, if not to *force* fortuitous discoveries to happen, at least to *increase the likelihood* that they happen sooner?

The answer is yes.

This exercise will help you to distinguish between the *problem* that you care about and *cases* of that problem, which might be multiple. If you can make this distinction, you will be better able to identify *your* Problem in other people's studies, especially by members of your Problem Collective who are not part of your Field and whose *cases* of your Problem might, on the surface, look utterly dissimilar.

Begin by writing down your research questions as specifically as you can, in whatever form they are currently in. Each question should contain as many of the following variables as possible:

- Time
- Place
- Agent/Subject
- Object
- Hypothesis

Here's a hypothetical example:

How did the Black Panther Party influence North American popular culture during the 1970s, if at all— and what does this influence or lack of influence tell us about popular culture of that era?

Overall, this is a solid question (even if it does rely for the time being on that slippery word "influence" that we discussed above) because it includes specifics for all of the above variables:

- Time: 1970s
- Place: North America
- Agent/Subject: Black Panther Party
- Object: [North American] popular culture
- Hypothesis: The subject had several cultural influences on the object during the time period; which were the most significant?

At the same time, however, it is not necessarily apparent what the *problem* is that drives this question, and thus what the Problem Collective is that the researcher would benefit from discovering. One could easily imagine this question being posed by a community activist, a comparative literature theorist, or a media studies scholar. The underlying "problem" here might pertain more to questions of media or of race or perhaps of the distinction between "popular" and "fine" arts and culture. Depending on what the real problem is here, any number of researcher communities might be the Problem Collective.

Starting with this formulation of the question, we can use a technique that involves changing the question methodically, one variable at a time. As we do so, we pay close attention to our own mental and emotional reactions to each permutation, to see how our attraction to or concern for the problem intensifies, diminishes, or remains unchanged.

Let's begin by changing the *place* variable:

> How did the Black Panther Party influence South African popular culture during the 1970s, if at all— and what does this influence or lack of influence tell us about South African popular culture of that era?

Did anything change inside you when you changed this one variable? What about the following:

> How did the Black Panther Party influence European popular culture during the 1970s, if at all—and what does this influence or lack of influence tell us about European popular culture of that era?

What happened this time? What about this:

> How did the Black Panther Party influence Soviet popular culture during the 1970s, if at all—and what does this influence or lack of influence tel! us about Soviet popular culture of that era?

Did anything change inside you when you changed this one variable? Did your excitement for the question dissipate or increase? Perhaps it hovered around the same level? And then comes the most important question of all: *Why?* Why does the history of the Black Panthers in, say, North America exert a powerful magnetic pull on you, but the same question posed about the Soviet Union, Europe, or South Africa falls short? This would imply that your concerns might fall less with the Black Panthers per se than with something about North America. If so, is there an aspect of your *real* question that you have yet to articulate? Are there missing pieces to your question—something that needs to be added to your question to make it a more faithful representation of your real concern? (Keep in mind: all answers to these questions provide useful "self-evidence" with which to orient your research.)

Now let's change the *place* variable back to its original setting, and change the *object* variable instead:

How did the Black Panther Party influence North American feminist movements during the 1970s, if at all—and what does this influence or lack of influence tell us about the feminist movements of that era?

Any change? How about the following:

How did the Black Panther Party influence North American filmmaking during the 1970s, if at all—and what does this influence or lack of influence tell us about film of that era?

What happened this time? Now how about this:

How did the Black Panther Party influence North American attitudes toward gun control during the 1970s, if at all—and what does this influence or lack of influence tell us about gun control debates of that era?

Every time you change one variable (and make sure to change *just one at a time*) the process is the same as before. Ask yourself: Better, worse, the same, and why?

Obviously, you'll need to use common sense in making substitutions. It would be meaningless to ask about the Black Panther Party's influence on North American popular culture during the 1950s, since the BPP was founded in 1966. Each substitution should result in a question that is meaningful and plausible. Skip those that seem absurd or untenable: some variables just cannot be changed. But if you *do* find yourself wondering about the influence of Black political movements on North American popular culture during the 1950s, perhaps your research question should *not* focus on the Black Panther Party, but on its antecedents.

Each time you change one variable, ask yourself these questions:

- Do I care more or less?
- Is something lost or gained?
- If I had to guess, *why* have things changed (or not)?
- Is the way I wrote my question as honest and comprehensive as it could be? Is this my *complete* question, or is it missing a variable?

Write down, next to each "changed variable," a few notes that capture what is going on inside your mind. Feel free to write briefly, or at length. Either way, make sure to record what happens to your interest each and every time a variable is changed.

As always, be honest with yourself. If, after changing a variable, you detect that you don't care anymore, or that something is lost, don't pretend to be concerned when you're not. If you are interested in the history of gender inequality in Spain, but *not* the history of gender inequality in Canada, just aim your research efforts in that direction.

On the other hand, perhaps you *are* interested—even excited about—gender inequality in *both* Spain *and* Canada. What this tells you is that your Problem is likely *not* primarily defined by geography, and so you may have many cases to choose from.

Imagine that your initial question centers on the history of child abuse in post–World War II Seattle. Say that the moment you change the variable *child* abuse to *elder* abuse your feeling of concern evaporates. *Is something wrong with me? Am I a bad person?* No. Honesty here might be uncomfortable, even painful, but you need to acknowledge to yourself (and any Sounding Boards) that, while as a human being and citizen of the world you are concerned with elder abuse, *as a researcher trying to identify your Problem* you are **not**. For any number of reasons, the problem that haunts you in life is particular and specific—*and this is entirely OK.* Write down this self-evidence and change a new variable.

By contrast, should you discover that the history of *both* child abuse *and* elder abuse concerns you equally, then this is a major clue that your primary concern might not be with any specific stage of life (childhood, adulthood, etc.), but rather with the lived experiences of, perhaps, populations or communities generally regarded as vulnerable.

To test out this possibility, we encourage you to invent *new variables* if you need to, either to be inserted into your revised question alongside the others already there, or perhaps to replace one already there. If the "stage of life" variable (child, elder, etc.) turns out to be potentially irrelevant, perhaps try different permutations with a variable about something like "condition of life" or "security level": *vulnerable, stable, invulnerable.*

Would you be equally interested in studying the history of child/elder abuse as, say, instances of abuse involving victims who are middle-aged, able-bodied, and who hail from a country's ethnonationally dominant group? If not, then this would seem to confirm the notion that "vulnerability" is not merely "interesting" to you, but the very heart of your research problem—in other words, that it *must* be present in any question you pose in order for you to feel satisfied and compelled.

After you've run through a series of permutations—by changing existing variables, or adding and playing with new variables, take stock of the process by categorizing all of your variables into these two categories. As always, do this in writing.

- *Negotiable or fungible variables.* These variables can be changed without influencing your level of interest. Perhaps for you, geography is negotiable or time period or the specific agents involved.
- *Non-negotiable variables.* These variables, when changed, lead to the evaporation of all interest, even when (ostensibly) your topic is still present. They have to be there.

Now comes the key step of producing self-evidence, the crucial moment of introspection that this entire exercise is preparing you to reflect on, in writing. Ask yourself these questions:

- When I see this list of negotiable versus non-negotiable variables, what does my *Problem* really seem to be?
- Why is it that I seem unconcerned with some variables being changed, while others seem sacred?
- When more than one "non-negotiable" is left over, which one is dominant?
- Which is the problem, and which is the case of the problem? Put another way, is X a case of Y, or is Y a case of X?
- Does my question, the way I first posed it, really capture my Problem, or is it simply a *case* of my Problem?

- If the latter, might there be a way for me to rephrase my question such that, while it remains as specific as before, it comes closer to articulating the core issues in my work?

This is not an instantaneous process, so go easy on yourself. You may not end up discovering your Problem right away through this experience. You can't force your mind to make such a profound discovery. But this exercise should bring additional clarity to the questions-to-problem work you did in chapter 2.

The key is to get yourself in the habit of assessing which variables matter most in your research questions. Get in this habit, and your mind will start to help you unconsciously. Long after your first pass at this "Change One Variable" exercise, your mind will continue to change the variables on its own—while you brush your teeth, while you walk to class or work, even while you sleep. You'll find discoveries happening much faster and more clearly than before.

The next step in that discovery process is to turn outward, and seek your Problem in the studies of other researchers. Now that you can distinguish between *problem* and *case of the problem*, you can identify kindred spirits in other fields. If you realize that your Problem is not limited by region, then expand your search to those who work on other parts of the world. The same is true for time period, discipline, and so on. Too many people, when trying to find their Problem Collective, limit their search to just one part of the bookstore, so to speak. Seek out members of your Problem Collective, using keyword searches and category searches. When you find a fellow Problem Collective member, look in their bibliography. Chances are you'll find more leads.

COMMONLY MADE MISTAKES
- Making substitutions that are far too small, and choosing new variables that are far too similar, to meaningfully test the importance of the variable to your research interests
- Skipping the steps of assessing which variables are negotiable (meaning that the revised question is of equal or greater interest to you than the original one) and which non-negotiable (meaning that your interest in the research question drops or disappears if you change the variable)
- Making substitutions that are impossible, illogical (e.g., anachronistic), or otherwise untenable because they are not supported by fact
- Not writing down your assessments of which variables are negotiable or non-negotiable
- Applying the problem/case distinction only to your work, instead of also using it to identify members of your Problem Collective in other fields

TRY THIS NOW: Before and After
The goals: *To identify the problem within a topic that most interests you by envisioning your research project within a larger problem-driven story. To then find other members of your Problem Collective who are contributing to that story.*

There is another way to accelerate the process of discovering your Problem and your Problem Collective. We call it the *Before and After Game*.

Imagine that the study you are working on—no matter its actual length or scope—were a single chapter in a book. What might the chapter *before* it be about? How about the chapter *after* it? And what would be the title of the book?

Here's a real-life example of what this game looks like in practice.

A student in Tom's Modern Chinese History class returned from the archives one afternoon, having encountered a compelling set of sources about the Boxer Uprising in China—a complex, tumultuous, and violent episode in early twentieth-century China that has riveted historians for decades. The sources practically "spoke for themselves," as the saying goes, recounting a harrowing story of a foreign missionary family living in China, fleeing the violence, hiding themselves in various locations, and ultimately losing a family member along the way—a young child, no less.

"I could tell a really compelling story about this," the student told Tom.

Unsurprisingly, the conversation between this student and Tom was full of words related to Chinese history. But the more the two of them spoke, the more that other words began to spill out—words that derived from the same primary sources, but which were suggestive of the student's curiosities and questions that went *beyond* the Boxer Uprising itself, and even China. Terms and phrases like "hiding," "refuge," "fleeing," and the "circulation of information during times of crisis."

Tom invited the student to play Before and After. At first, the two tried out the most obvious possibility: that the hypothetical book the student would write would be about the Boxer Rebellion itself. In this line of thinking, the chapter that the student was writing would be the "one about missionaries." The chapters before and after, therefore, might focus on, say, "Chinese laborers during the Boxer Uprising" or perhaps "foreign diplomats during the Boxer Uprising." *Is this what you have in mind?* Tom asked the student. *As I narrate this imaginary table of contents to you, are you getting more excited or less? Does it enliven you, or does it leave you lifeless?*

Lifeless, the student answered, without hesitation. This was not the main problem that they found compelling.

So they tried again. What if the book was called something like *Hiding in China: A Cultural History*, Tom speculated. *Perhaps the chapter before or after might not be about the Boxers at all, but on other cases of crisis, refuge, and flight in modern Chinese history. Perhaps the preceding chapter might be called "Hiding from the Taiping Rebels," focused on refuge and flight during China's mid-nineteenth-century civil war, the Taiping Rebellion. And perhaps the chapter that follows might be titled "Hiding on the Korean Peninsula: War Refugees during the First Sino-Japanese War, 1894–1895."*

A little bit better, the student responded. Still, hesitation.

What if the word "China" didn't show up in the book title at all? *What if the book was about a cultural history of hiding, focused on times of war and conflict, but not limited geographically to Asia or any other specific part of the world? In that hypothetical universe, the following chapter might take place in South Africa, during the Boer War, or elsewhere.*

Yes! Suddenly, signs of life returned to the student's face. This was getting closer to the student's problem.

The point of the Before and After Game is *not* that your Problem should "become" the one recommended by your Sounding Board—that would be fatal. Do not "settle" for a suggestion, even a well-meaning one. Neither is the goal of the exercise to dramatically expand the research project to include an immense number of additional, complex case studies.

Rather, the goal is to set in motion a thought process in which the researcher begins to examine *and reexamine* their questions from multiple perspectives and in multiple dimensions. Once a researcher learns how to carry out this exercise for themselves, without necessarily talking to a mentor or a Sounding Board, they will be equipped to oversee the brainstorming process independently, rapidly iterating an untold number of imaginary tables of contents and book titles. Eventually, one of these ideas will "catch," and the researcher will understand what they are *really after*.

Now it's your turn. Follow these steps:

1. Envision your study as a chapter in a research book focused on your Problem.
2. Write down a sentence describing your study, as best you can summarize it. Use this as a placeholder title for your "current chapter"—the project you are actually working on.
3. Now imagine a logical progression of a broader, book-length study delving into your Problem: What would be the titles of the chapters that precede and follow yours? Write down a chapter title for each of them. If you want to go further, think of what additional chapters of this hypothetical book might focus on.
4. Give that book a compelling and descriptive title.
5. Now come up with at least two (and ideally more) alternate scenarios. Repeat the above steps, coming up with titles for the current chapter, the preceding chapter, the next chapter, and the book.

6. For each hypothetical book, fill in a chart like the one shown in table 8.

TABLE 8. PLAY BEFORE AND AFTER

Book title: _____
Preceding chapter: _____
Current chapter: _____
Next chapter: _____
Excitement level: _____ (low/medium/high)
Why this response? _____ (Here, take as much space as you need to assess, describe, and speculate about how and why you responded the way you did to this envisioned scenario.)

You can benefit from this exercise whether you are writing a term paper for a class over a few weeks or working on a much larger project, like a graduate thesis or a book, since it forces you to think through *your orientation* within the vast world of a topic, and to make sure that your approach is driven by your Problem.

As always, pay close attention to how you yourself respond to the scenario, and get your thoughts down *in writing*. Get that EKG machine back out, and hook yourself back up. Do any of these hypothetical books call out to you more than others? Why do you think this is? Are there any "obvious" book titles that, for whatever reason, *don't* speak to you? Why might this be? How might this help you refine or revise the way in which you are describing your research project to others, and to yourself?

Answering these questions gets you, again, closer to your Problem. But it also helps you to envision, in a problem-driven way, how your current research project in the making might intersect with other conversations. As in the *cultural history of hiding during times of war* example, the case represented by the primary source was related to China, but the problem was not, and this opened up many possibilities. Use your results from Before and

After to think about the directions you might go beyond your Field to find members of your Problem Collective. Write them down, and start searching.

COMMONLY MADE MISTAKES
- Talking yourself into "liking" a hypothetical project that your mentor suggests or that seems to be the "obvious" choice because it is related to the topic. Avoid the power of suggestion, and trust your instincts. If you find yourself hesitating, take note of that.
- Ignoring an instinctual feeling of disinterest or boredom in a hypothetical project, or not taking the time to consider *why* you feel aversion to a potential project choice. Dislikes can be instructive.
- Based on this envisioning exercise, feeling like you need to undertake a major project whose scope is far beyond what you can realistically accomplish. Remember that the goal is to pinpoint the problem that excites you so that you can find other members of your Problem Collective. Again: write, search, write!

TRY THIS NOW:
Map Out Your Collective (Secondary Source Search)
The goal: *To use one secondary source from your Problem Collective to find many more Problem Collective sources.*

Now that you've completed the "Change One Variable" and the "Before and After" exercises, you are in a great position to venture out and actively search for your Collective. In "Change One Variable," you identified which variables in your question are optional, negotiable, and fungible, and which are absolutely essential and non-negotiable. Likewise, even though you feel compelled by your question the way it is currently articulated, nevertheless the "Change One Variable" exercise revealed that there are certain other variables that, while you may not end up researching them, would also be compelling to you—suggesting that the boundaries of your Problem may be more expansive than what your question might suggest.

Now is the time to put this hard-won self-awareness to work by running new keyword searches—this time in a search for *secondary* sources. If your question focuses on the history of child abuse in Seattle (to use our previous example), and yet you would be equally interested perhaps in studying the same topic in Toronto, Turkey, or Tel Aviv, then go ahead and try to find studies carried out in other geographic locales. Read those works, and see how you feel as you read them. Are they enlightening? Does your EKG reading spike?

And if you know, by way of the "Change One Variable" exercise, that you could also imagine yourself doing work on elder abuse, go ahead and run searches for this topic as well. Get your hands on these books, articles, documentaries, works of art, and more. What happens when you read these materials?

Just like the very first exercise in the book—"Search Yourself"—your objective here is twofold:

1. To read these Problem Collective books and articles, understand their arguments, and take notes
2. To *read yourself as you read Problem Collective sources*, to see what kind of impact, if any, these works are having on you

If they are not having an impact on you, then this gives you a clue that perhaps this author, however interesting their research is, might not be part of your Problem Collective. But if you do notice your pulse quickening, and your mind racing with new questions, this suggests that perhaps you have made a discovery after all—*even if the book or article in your hands seems to have nothing to do with your case*.

We cannot tell you when this discovery will happen, how long it will take, or if it has indeed taken place. Only you can answer these questions. But we will tell you this: if you have been working through all of the exercises in this book so far, and if you have been producing and analyzing all of the necessary self-evidence, chances are high that, by this point, you have the requisite skills of introspection and self-awareness. And this self-awareness—this work of taking notice of yourself, trusting yourself, writing "self-evidence" down on paper, analyzing it, and then deciding your next steps based upon your new insights—will accelerate the process of discovering your Problem Collective.

And remember: it only takes the discovery of *one* book, *one* article, *one* documentary, or *one* lecture to throw the doors wide open.

Truly, once you discover even one piece of writing by a member of your Collective, from there the process of discovering other members—dozens, hundreds—becomes easier and faster. Every new study that deals with your Problem will also yield further sources in its footnotes, endnotes, and bibliography. Read the table of contents, the abstract, the introduction, the conclusion. Skim the body of the text. Comb through the footnotes and the bibliography. Take note of any title that jumps out at you, *no matter whether or not this work has any surface-level connection to your case*. Indeed, the fact that these books and articles *don't* deal with the exact same thing as you—the same place, person, or time period—is precisely the point. That distance helps clarify that the problem you are so passionate about is not limited to a time and place but, rather, is shared by researchers working on very different topics.

Add all of these sources to your own research bibliography, then get your hands on every one of them you can, and go through the same process with each of those new sources. Repeat this process until you feel confident that you have made enough connections to begin some serious reading, starting with the most promising works. And as you read through these works more closely, and as you discover the ones that really do seem to be tapped into the same problem as you, ask yourself the following questions over and over:

- What does this author call my Problem?
- What is this author's word for the thing that disturbs me?
- What vocabulary does this author, who clearly seems to be kept awake at night by the same gnawing question as I am, use to describe themself, whether professionally, intellectually, or otherwise?

Write down the answers to these questions. Indeed, write down anything that comes to mind, because this is a rare and joyous moment: the moment when you find your fellow travelers. These are the people who are going to help you, inspire you, validate you, challenge you, and enable you to find your voice.

COMMONLY MADE MISTAKES
- Not using the results of the "Change One Variable" exercise in this keyword search
- Dismissing your instinctual feeling of interest in or attraction to a secondary source because, on the

surface, it doesn't appear to be directly related to your case
- Not writing down your answers to the three questions about how the secondary sources you find describe or define your Problem
- Giving up early, or not repeating the process of analysis and introspection with multiple secondary sources
- Only examining secondary sources that are in your Field, meaning that you likely have not significantly changed your variables in the "Change One Variable" exercise

Rewriting for Your Collective

Now that you've found your Problem Collective, the next challenge is to *write for them* — or, really, to *rewrite* for them. We encourage you to try this out using your draft research proposal from chapter 3, but you can also apply the same techniques to any other piece of research writing you have in draft form, such as an essay, an abstract, a conference paper, an article, or a grant proposal — even a speech or presentation.

This process begins with two steps:

1. Identifying the Field jargon you may currently be using (perhaps unconsciously) to talk about your Problem
2. Eliminating this "insider" language from the description of your Problem so as to make things comprehensible to people outside your Field in language they'll understand

Rewriting for your Problem Collective is not as simple as it sounds. Consider these three challenges. First, members of your Collective may know little to nothing about your subject matter. They may know nothing about your time period, your subjects, your region. They may be entirely ignorant of your Field, and they certainly won't appreciate its jargon — a point we'll return to in a minute.

Second, the things that impress your Field might not impress your Collective. Maybe their Field answered those questions already. Maybe they have a different consensus about how free will operates in democratic societies, or about which environmental threats to the planet are the most pressing. Maybe scholar X's study launched a thousand dissertations in your Field but is virtually unknown to your Collective. Or, for whatever reason, members of your Collective simply find the preoccupations of your Field . . . well . . . *not* preoccupying.

Third, your Field's hang-ups and taboos don't concern your Collective. One faction in your Field claims that freedom fighters brought about that regime change; another insists that the government was toppled by terrorists. Your Field agrees that you should never question the validity of theory Y, or should always refer to subject Z with a certain nomenclature, but your Collective has no such inhibitions. You might well discover later that members of your Collective are weighed down by *other* baggage. But, in any case, you are likely going to have to write for your Collective in ways that your Field doesn't demand of you.

What your Collective will demand is that you keep the problem front and center. Freed of your Field's bugbears, you can stay focused on the problem you're trying to solve. It should drive the flow of your prose, the structure of your argument, and the words you use.

Every field has its own shorthand, its thieves' cant — the jargon that makes outsiders either wince or go blank. You can't talk that way to your Collective. You simply won't make yourself understood. This is one of the reasons that finding your Problem Collective is so important: to make connections, you have to step out of your Field's echo chamber.

Imagine you have to miss art class one day and ask your friend to video-record the class session for you. Unfortunately, your friend ends up recording only the audio, and what you hear the instructor saying is this:

> *As you can see on the left side of this painting, the second figure is looking menacingly at the figure here. But over here, we can see that the figure's expression is placid. Take note of this, because we will return to it.*

You'd be lost, and for good reason.

For people *inside* the room, pointing at things while speaking about them is a natural and effective way to communicate. People *outside* of the room, however — including smart people — will struggle to make sense of it. Which painting is the instructor pointing at? Who is on the left side? Who is the second figure? Where is "over here"?

"Pointing-while-speaking" is essentially what all of us are doing when we write as if addressing *only* members of our Field.

Consider the following sentence:

> *After a brutal civil war between the GMD and the CCP, the latter emerged victorious, going on to form the PRC.*

To a historian of modern China, the sentence above is completely straightforward. For everyone outside that field, the sentence looks like secret code. It conceals rather than reveals.

So, when writing for your Collective, start by killing your acronyms:

> *After a brutal civil war between the Nationalist Party of China (Guomindang) and the Chinese Communist Party, the latter emerged victorious, going on to form the People's Republic of China.*

Here's a made-up example of another type of Field writing that keeps everyone else (and perhaps even some Field members) outside the room:

The findings of Park and Williams refute Wendell's influential hypothesis.

Rephrase to bring your Collective inside:

The excavation of tenth-century Norwegian graves containing knives and forks alongside humpback whale bones disproves one scholar's influential hypothesis that Vikings ate only shrimp.

So *that's* what you were talking about!

Insider language is of course valuable — even essential — in certain contexts. Used among experts, it eliminates redundancy and speeds the conversation, allowing them more time to delve deeply into the more complex aspects of their work. You do not want a thoracic surgeon to explain every specialist term. Nor do you want the operating room to be populated by those who need things explained in lay terms.

Insider language is, nevertheless, anathema to the early phases of the research process. Unlike the emergency room, where life-or-death decisions must be made rapidly and efficiently, the early phases of research benefit from *slowing down and decompressing language.* Translating from specialist to lay language is a necessary part of writing for your Collective.

The reasons are simple. As you already know, the people in your Collective will likely not hail from your same Field or share your same topic. They will share the underlying problems and disturbances that motivate your research, but they will simply not know what your Field-specific code words mean. This includes not just nouns, but also verbs like "intervene" and "negotiate," which — especially when used in a metaphorical sense — often beg the questions of *what* exactly is being done, and *how*. Replace those terms with a full description — gloss them so as to equip your fellow Collective members with the basic information they need in order to make sense of your research orientation. Help them to understand your questions and recognize you as part of the same Problem Collective. Express your question, problem, or disturbance with reference to specific places, time periods, personages, and institutions.

Give them the context, and they will be able to help you push your work further. Remove acronyms, abbreviations, and shorthands so that a fellow Collective member can share ideas or pose questions that stress-test your assumptions and help lead you to a breakthrough.

TRY THIS NOW:
Find and Replace All "Insider Language"
The goals: *To identify language in your writing that make sense only to members of your Field and to rewrite so that you can connect with members of your Problem Collective.*

We highly recommend that you do this exercise not on the computer but on paper, using a set of highlighters, preferably in at least five colors. The exercise involves three steps.

Step 1: Read your Field writing with Collective eyes

Print out a copy of your draft research proposal, and then highlight every instance of "insider language" you can find. Use different colors for different types of insider language, for example:

- Blue, for every time a person is mentioned by surname only, or without any introduction when first mentioned
- Red, for jargon and technical terminology that is presented without definition or explanation
- Orange, for any adjectives or adverbs that obscure more than they reveal
- Green, for every event that is referenced but not identified or explained briefly
- Yellow, for acronyms

You can create your own categories as well.

If you choose to do this exercise on the computer, you can color-code using a text highlighting tool. We recommend using colors because doing so makes the patterns in your language obvious at a glance. ("So much yellow—I'm clearly overusing acronyms!") But you can also make such distinctions using different fonts, notations (numbers, letters, symbols), or any mark-up code that suits you.

The figure below provides an example in monochrome. A page that starts out looking like the one on the left will end up looking like the one on the right.

There is no prize for producing the cleanest page. Now is the time to find and flag as much of this insider language as possible, as doing so will help you to sharpen your thinking about how to communicate more effectively with your Collective.

Step 2: Rewrite your way out of your Field

Now that you have annotated your document, rewrite just those parts that you've highlighted. For each, do the following at first mention:

a. **Individual.** Provide the full name, preferably with a brief biographical description.
b. **Institution.** Describe it in sufficient detail.
c. **Technical term.** Remove and replace with a description of the phenomenon or principle. If it is necessary to retain the term, define it.
d. **Adjectives and adverbs.** Find any words that are secretly trying to "smuggle in" judgment statements—words like *traditionally*, *normal*, *obviously*, *scientifically*, *clearly*, and *irrational*—and replace them with language that is more specific, open-ended, and transparent.

BEFORE

AFTER

JARGON

UNEXPLAINED EVENTS

UNHELPFUL ADVERBS & ADJECTIVES

e **Event.** Briefly explain what happened, and any relevant context.

f. **Acronym.** Remove and replace with the full name, or a brief description.

Remember, the overarching goal is not just to *avoid obscuring* things, but also to *demonstrate what needs to be demonstrated.* Your commitment is affirmative.

COMMONLY MADE MISTAKES

- Neglecting to highlight obscure or Field-specific adjectives, adverbs, and verbs, in addition to the obvious nouns
- Using only one highlighting color (or font or notation style or other unique identifying mark-up technique), instead of several, which can help you more systematically and precisely identify your habits of using insider language
- Replacing Field terms with different Field terms, instead of with language comprehensible to a nonspecialist

SOUNDING BOARD:
Does the Lay Version of My Proposal Make Sense?
Now that you've systematically identified all of the various types of insider language in your research proposal, replace those terms with language that could be understood by a lay (nonexpert) reader. Then ask someone who is not a subject matter expert (i.e., someone who possesses no specialized knowledge of your topic) to read that version of your proposal and highlight any parts that don't make sense to them. You might be surprised: when we

get close to our subject matter, it's easy to lose perspective. Which words or phrases do they find confusing? Can they follow the logic? Which passages puzzle them? Rewrite those sections until they become clear. Your Sounding Board can help you to express your research problem more clearly.

Welcome to Your Collective

Note that we do not call this group a Solution Collective. Members of a Problem Collective might differ radically in how they think the problem can or should be solved. What is the solution to poverty? What is an ideal preschool education? How best to deter terrorism? Proposals vary, but a self-centered researcher can take in stride differences of opinion within their Problem Collective. You can accept with equanimity (rather than defensiveness) that not everyone in your Collective thinks like you. Not all of them are or will become your friends. And this is a good thing. You are not looking for confirmation of your preexisting ideas. You are not looking for sympathy. Rather, you are looking for new perspectives on the problem that motivates you. The self-centered researcher is able to consider various proposed solutions, and methods of finding solutions, with open-minded critical detachment.

Don't dwell. A Problem Collective is a collective body of ideas, and ideas are mobile and fluid. It is an evolving place to seek new ideas, or to recharge and renew. It is not a refuge in which to hide from your Field or seek validation. Nor is the purpose of finding your Collective to overawe people with your intellectual breadth or interdisciplinarity—such conceit is anathema to Self-Centered Research. The idea is to be searching. You should constantly be leaving (and often returning to) your Problem Collective, setting out into other regions, categories, time periods, and so forth. And remember that this is just a beginning. You might well belong to more than one Problem Collective, and your allegiances may shift from project to project.

5. How to Navigate Your Field

· ·

Finding your Problem Collective is difficult. Finding your Field is simple. Your Field finds you.

The main reason for that is because fields are typically connected to topics, in the broadest sense, and those categories make a claim on you. Your Field pulls you back into Topic Land.

Fields have their own journals, professional associations, newsletters, and myriad other institutional apparatuses that call out to interested parties. Universities are organized into departments, most of which are named after fields, like chemistry, economics, computer science, classics, English, or Asian studies. A School of Population Studies or an Institute of Gender Studies might be organized by collective, but these modes of organization are more rare in most institutional settings. The field-collective dynamic is part of the ongoing push and pull of intellectual life in the modern academy.

A field is different from a Problem Collective in that it is defined by a scope of activity or research targets. A collective is defined by a shared intellectual agenda or array of concerns. If your research project is on the history of the cuckoo clock, you are unavoidably part of the field of Germanic studies, given that timepiece's connections to the Black Forest, but your Problem Collective might be scholars of material culture or the history of technology.

Or let's say you're in a Department of Art History and you want to write about the contemporary artist Xu Bing, known for his installation *Book from the Sky*, made up of scrolls printed with over 4,000 "fake" Chinese characters. You might find yourself talking to linguists, curators, calligraphers, graphic artists, computer scientists, historians of woodblock printing technology, scholars of script cultures, or scholars of "nonsense" poetry. Among them, your intellectual kindred might be people curious about how and why artists use familiar cultural forms to challenge expectations about aesthetics and intelligibility.

Your Collective is like your friends: you share interests and you choose to spend time with them. Finding your Collective is a process of self-affiliation. Your Field is more like your family: the senior members existed before you did, they claim you as one of their own, and — like it or not — you live with them and have to spend a lot of time in their company. Your membership in a field is not entirely a matter of choice, as it's partly assigned to you. You can of course renounce your Field, spurn its values and conventions, but people might still remark upon the resemblance.

People tend to view their families through their own identities. Some never realize that their family members have other identities too — *as members of other collectives*. Children don't always think about their parents' engagement with their profession; they take it for granted that a parent goes to work and then comes home to play with them or pick them up from school. But the parent may spend many or most of their waking hours working on problems that have nothing to do with their child. They may participate in institutional cultures, associations, voluntary affiliations, advocacy groups, or other organizations whose reason for being is to solve a problem the child might not even be aware of. When we discover that our parents have been spending so much time working on something else, besides raising us, we see them in a new light and ask: *Who are these people, really?*

One of the central question of this chapter is this: How do you deal with the differing problems and interests of members of your Field?

Why, when they do their own research, do members of your Field not necessarily write for you? As you now realize, they are likely writing for their Problem Collective. If you wish that your Field would strive to know you on your own terms — to know what *your* Problem is — stop to ask yourself: What's *their* Problem? After all, for institutions it is the *field* that comes first. And yet, for the scholars who make up any specific field, it is their *Problems* that come first. This is one of the internal contradictions that make fields both dynamic and frustrating places to be.

Your Collective helps you to *get to you.*

Your Field helps you to *outgrow yourself.*

Identify the different Problem Collectives within your Field and you'll understand better how your Field works, and how to make your Field work for you. Being a member of a field isn't just getting a membership card and becoming a passive conduit of its values and conventions. You get a role in helping the field to evolve.

Find the Problems within Your Field

Fields have multiple advantages, including topical coherence, and various institutional structures such as journals, conferences, associations, bibliographies, and funding bodies that support research and learning in a particular area. These institutional structures make it easier to find sources, facts, and other researchers connected to a topic. They continually produce and codify knowledge, establish and refine conventions, and perform quality control on the research output of their members through peer review. Problem Collectives lack these supports, and that is one of the reasons they are so much harder to identify and connect with.

Fields also have limitations whose effects on the researcher range in severity from inconvenient to debilitating.

As they develop conventions, they also grow blind spots. Received wisdom can devolve into cant and discourage innovation. Doctrines can emerge, due to undue deference to — or self-promotion by — authority. Junior researchers may feel like they have to follow the herd, and reflexively suppress their own interests and ideas.

Much of the work you did in part 1 of this book to become a self-centered researcher has prepared you to overcome or avoid these common pitfalls. Again and again, whether working with a single source, an array of search results, or just pen and paper, you have been listening to yourself and been honest about when you feel that visceral current of electricity.

In this chapter, we offer several ideas and methods for the following:

- Navigating a vast field of knowledge efficiently, while never losing sight of your Problem
- Making best use of the resources of your Field, especially members of your Field who are *also* members of your Problem Collective
- Avoiding common traps — conceptual and methodological — that researchers fall into in interacting with their field

Among those mistakes is to view a field as a topic that is merely a collection of subfields, or subtopics, that are more specific and thus have less to do with one another. Again and again, we have seen students think to themselves: *I just need to "narrow down" my topic — then I'll have a project.* But, as we said before: *You cannot narrow your way out of Topic Land.* (And Subtopic Land is worse.)

This is why we encourage you to view your Field not as a collection of subfields but rather an assortment of Problem Collectives. Adopting this mindset allows you to look beyond the specific *cases* to see the *problems* shared by researchers working on radically different topics. You will learn to take advantage of the incredible resources of a field without getting trapped in Topic Land.

Make this mental shift, and you will fundamentally alter your relationship with your Field.

Read Your Field for *Their* Problems: Reimagining the "Literature Review"

Let's start by rethinking a common way of navigating a field: the "literature review."

The "lit review," as it's often known, is a required component of academic theses, articles, dissertations, and books. This is the section near the front of a thesis or article where the author asks and answers the question "How did we get here, to the problem at hand?" ("State of the field" articles have a similar agenda: to synthesize ideas and analyze their research implications.) A literature review establishes your authority to conduct a study by demonstrating that you have read all of the relevant studies on a particular topic or problem. You trace the threads of an intellectual genealogy, identifying the debates, theories, revelations, and transformative ideas necessary for a reader to appreciate the agenda of *your* study. You are not just compiling a chronology or a list of publications. You are making an argument that your research extends from or builds on those earlier efforts and addresses a new part of the problem.

In chapter 2 we advised against justifying your project by claiming that it fills a "gap in the field." Now we will show you how not to be a gap filler. A field, after all, is not a leaky dam that needs a hole plugged to keep it from collapsing, or a garment that needs mending. It is more like an ongoing conversation at a party that you have just joined, and no one will be impressed if you just take up space. What they want from you is ideas, expressed in an engaging fashion, that will help improve their own ideas.

Literature reviews are notorious for being a boring slog. They're hard to write and sometimes even harder to read. And for you, they might now be even harder. Having just read several studies by other members of your Collective — works that inspire you because they speak directly to the core of your Problem — you might feel less than excited to read across an entire field, including parts of it that are remote from your project. It can feel like the intellectual equivalent of doing one's taxes — a duty, rather than a pleasure.

Fortunately, there is a simple way to remedy this feeling. Given that every field is made up of researchers from different Problem Collectives, your job in the lit review is to listen to these other collectives, to acknowledge how members of other collectives bring their own agendas and values to bear on your topic, and to consider their findings in the light of *their* Problems (not yours).

Interacting with other collectives gives you a better sense of your own values. You learn to respect other collectives, and to avoid the mistake of thinking that if someone is asking different questions about the same topic that they're simply wrong. It may be that they just have a different agenda and are trying to solve a different problem.

Consider this scenario: you're at a conference for your Field and you are watching a presentation that pertains to your topic of research — and you find it boring.

A thought immediately crosses your mind: *This colleague is dealing with my Problem, but poorly.*

This is a "selfish" response, not a self-centered one. For a self-centered researcher who is aware of Problem Collectives, the response instead would be, *This colleague seems to be dealing with the same topic as me, but through the lens of a very different problem than mine. I wonder what their Problem is?*

A new set of questions emerges: *How might their work, and their Problem, help me and mine — and vice versa? Are there things they're seeing that I'm not?*

The advantages of the latter approach are obvious: you'll be better able to harness the productive friction between field and collective to create new energy, and to change them both.

These are the processes that can enliven the blandly titled "literature review." Your job in navigating your Field is to bring together scholars, some who are just entering the profession and others who are long dead, into conversation with one another about a set of questions and concerns that together add up to a survey of the most compelling and important research on your Problem.

Here are a few things to keep in mind when evaluating sources, which apply equally to those written by members of your Field and your Collective:

- **Be skeptical.** Just because something was published in a peer-reviewed journal or a book doesn't mean it's watertight. You shouldn't be groundlessly contrarian, but neither should you take the words of experts at face value.
- **Be fair.** Represent every source's merits and shortcomings accurately.
- **Focus on the author's concerns, not your own.** When you write an evaluation of a particular piece of writing, focus on the points of greatest salience to the author, not to you. In other words, focus on what they were trying to achieve in writing this study instead of selfishly scavenging it for parts. There is nothing quite so unfair as a review that heaps criticism on points that were, in fact, of minor significance to the author's main goals.

Think of your Field as less a set of commandments to be followed uncritically than a set of propositions to be tested, refined, modified, reordered, and added to. This is where you come in.

Be skeptical, but avoid the rookie mistake of scoffing at

the authorities just for the thrill of it. The satirical weekly *The Onion* captured this tendency with the title of a fictional book: Wendel Spencer's *Schools Are* Not *Failing Our Children: How We Took a Commonly Held Opinion and Declared the Opposite*. Your Field does not need more posers.

Likewise, a field does not (or should not) tolerate people who bully or harangue their colleagues. In contests of ideas, it's the ideas that matter, not their proponents. When you are evaluating a source, keep your focus on the research, not on the researcher. Doing so will help keep you unprejudiced, and you'll have no qualms about giving praise or censure where it's due. It's always incumbent on you to represent other people's ideas in good faith.

TRY THIS NOW:
Start Your Own "What's Your Problem?" Bookstore (aka Organize Your Field into Problem Collectives)

The goal: *To sort studies in your Field by the problems that motivate instead of the topic they are "about," by arranging a small number of secondary sources into "problem sections."*

In chapter 4, we asked you to imagine a bookstore where the shelves are organized according to the problems that propel each of the authors' books, not the "topics" each book is about. Instead of a section named, let's say, Philosophy—with books about German philosophers on one shelf, Greek philosophers on another, Indian philosophers on a third, and so on—this "Problem Bookstore" would have sections called (again, let's say) *How can humans authenticate religious scripture or other works from antiquity?* Or perhaps *How to make sense of evil?* Or maybe *How can we teach ourselves and others to act morally?*

Well, the time for hypotheticals is over. Now your job is make this bookstore a reality (albeit on a small scale) using the books you plan to read for your research. Here are the steps:

1. Choose six to eight short secondary sources (articles or book chapters—not entire books) in your Field related to your topic. By this point in your research, you have compiled a preliminary bibliography of studies on your topic. Your Sounding Board has probably made some suggestions as well. Don't fret too much over the selection of studies. As long as they are serious works of scholarship, and as long as they are "about" your topic, that's all you need. You can always add more later.

2. Using table 9 as a model, write down the *topic* of the first study in your list. Here is the place where you can write generalities, such as "ancient Greek philosophy" or "Buddhism." This should be pretty straightforward. You should be able to identify the topic even before reading the study, using the introduction of the article or chapter (or even just the title).

3. Now write down the specific *case* that the study focuses on. Perhaps it's a study of medieval Buddhist architecture in Japan, or a specific element of ancient Stoic philosophy. Again, this should be pretty simple, since the case will likely be mentioned in the title or the opening pages of the study.

4. List the specific questions that the study poses. Here is where things get more precise, and where your close reading skills will pay off. Just as you did earlier with your own research—where you

brainstormed and refined a host of small- and medium-scale questions that together started to "add up" to a broader project—here is where you try to identify the small- and medium-scale questions that comprise the study you're reading. If you're lucky, the researcher will articulate their questions clearly and explicitly. But you might have to "reverse engineer" the author's questions, based on the explanations they are providing, and the claims they are making. Identify as many questions as you can, striving to find *at least* ten.

5. Try to identify *patterns* among those questions. Once again, this part of the process is exactly the same exercise that you did before, only this time you're focusing on someone else's work, rather than your own. Analyze the list of the ten-plus questions you've found, and ask yourself: *If I had to venture a guess, what does this author seem to be concerned about or preoccupied with? What seems to be driving them?* Pay attention as well to the questions that the author *doesn't* seem to be asking—questions which, for you, seem like obvious ones, but which don't seem to be addressed in the study. All of this is "self-evidence"—remember that?—only this time, the "self" in question is not you, but *them*.

6. Try to identify the *problem*. Now that you've created an inventory of questions, and analyzed the patterns that comprise those questions, you're ready for the hardest but most rewarding part of this exercise: to try and see *past* the author's case study, and identify the deeper-seated problem. Write down a one-sentence description of this problem *in as general terms as possible*. It goes

without saying, we hope, but be sure to avoid conflating the author's *case* with their *Problem*.

7. Repeat steps 1 through 6 for the other studies in your list.
8. Once you have completed this process for most or all of your studies, try to identify any themes or patterns that connect the different authors' Problems. Do any of the different problems you've identified seem related somehow? If not, don't try to force things. It's OK if there are "one-of-a-kind" questions. But if there are ones that seem to share something in common, try to group them together. Now try to give a name to these broader Problem Collectives (you may need to adjust your description, broadening or abstracting it a bit, which is OK). The groups you end up creating—and the names you give to them—will become the sections of your Problem Bookstore. Once you have them, you're ready to open your shop and welcome fellow seekers!

TABLE 9. ORGANIZE YOUR FIELD INTO PROBLEM COLLECTIVES

SOURCE #	STUDY TITLE	TOPIC	CASE	PROBLEM	PROBLEM COLLECTIVE
1					
2					
3					
4					
5					
6					

The point of this exercise is twofold. First, as you learn to sort your Field into different Problem Collectives, you will become far more efficient at navigating your Field, and far better at understanding (and remembering) the arguments and facts you've read. When you know the problem that motivates someone's work, not only do you gain clarity about *how* you should be reading that work (e.g., discerning which parts are key to a person's argument, and which parts are mere side notes), but you also have a much clearer sense of where in your own brain you should be storing and organizing all of the arguments and information you're encountering. A scholar's problem is the architecture of their argument, the skeletal structure, the grid. Without it, reading even the most rigorous work of scholarship can sometimes feel like being overwhelmed by a tsunami of facts and arguments.

There's a second reason, as well: you'll develop a kind of magical power, the ability to connect with fellow researchers on a deeper, more meaningful level, by seeing what they are *really* working on, rather than just the place, time period, and so on where their research in based. What you are going to find is that two genealogical studies of (let's say) the exact same Middle Eastern royal family, or three sociological studies of the exact same favela in Rio de Janeiro, may be motivated by *entirely different problems*. Similarly, one study about Rio may be propelled by the *exact same problem* as one about a Middle Eastern royal family. Cases and problems are *not* the same thing.

To be clear, as your list of secondary sources grows for your project, we are not advocating that you make an exhaustive catalogue or a comprehensive re-sorting of every study in your field. (You're not *really* starting a bookstore.) But we do believe that this mindset leads to a much more effective (and, frankly, enjoyable) research process. Simply put, knowing the problem at stake, whether in your own work or in the work of another, makes navigating the ocean of studies easier.

COMMONLY MADE MISTAKES
- Sorting studies by topic or subtopic, instead of by problem
- Sorting studies by case, instead of by problem

TRY THIS NOW: Change *Their* Variables

The goals: *To gain an understanding of how topics, problems, and cases of problems work for other researchers. To learn about the research problem of a mentor, Sounding Board, or peer by interviewing them using the "Change One Variable" exercise from above.*

Distinguishing between the problem and the case that exemplifies the problem can be difficult. You've probably discovered this while doing the previous exercises. You'll also have realized why seeing beyond the case to the problem is so valuable, and why it is helpful to have multiple strategies for doing so.

This exercise turns the tables on "Change One Variable." In chapter 4, you changed one variable at a time in your *own* research question to see what this revealed about your Problem. Now, you are going to ask another researcher—a mentor, Sounding Board, or peer—to do the same thing aloud with you so that you can learn more about their topic, their case, and their Problem.

If that person is in your Field, great—you'll learn about how the topic-problem-case dynamic affects someone else working on similar subject matter. But this is purely optional. The key thing is to learn how to pinpoint the driving problems in the research world outside your own mind. This process should be empowering, and strengthen the bond between you and a fellow researcher.

Here's what to do:

1. Give yourself a refresher on how the "Change One Variable" (COV) exercise works. You've covered a lot since you did it yourself, so reread that part of chapter 4.

2. Introduce the exercise to your chosen interviewee in a way that presumes no prior knowledge on their part of how the COV exercise works. You can describe the goal and the procedure to them yourself, or just give them an opportunity to read it in the book. Explain that, having gone through COV yourself, you'd now like to interview them about their research, using the same technique. Explain that this interview is part of your own self-training. In addition to learning more about their research, you also want to practice distinguishing topics from cases from problems in other people's research. Make it clear that this conversation is confidential, and that you will be taking notes only for yourself.

3. Prepare for an informal and nonjudgmental conversation. Your job is to listen, to ask clarification questions, and to write things down. You're already experienced with writing self-evidence; now you'll be the stenographer writing down the self-evidence of someone else. Bring pens and notepads and—don't forget—the list on page 131 to keep track of which variables changed and how your interviewee responded to each change.

4. Start things off by asking questions that prompt your interviewer to identify their topic, and then produce a question *containing all of the relevant variables* that they think best encapsulate their core problem. For example:
   - What do you work on? (Topic) (NOTE: If their response is "I work on lots of things!" just have them choose one representative project for starters.)
   - If you had to put what you work on into a question, what would that be? (NOTE: If they produce a *nonquestion* ["I work on the question of poverty"—see page 47], tell them that this exercise requires a real question. Give them an example from COV, if necessary, or ask them to choose a question from one of their studies.)
5. Write down their description of their topic and their full research question. Take your time here— read the question back to them and ask if it's complete. Remind them that the rules of the game require the question to be as comprehensive as possible, and include all of the relevant variables. It does not have to be elegant.
6. Once they confirm that the question is complete, *you* start changing variables for them, one by one, and writing down the results. *How did this variable change affect your EKG—your level of excitement? If you had to guess, why?* This is the meat of the exercise, which will take the most time and—in order to work—require that you let *nothing* slip past your Noticing radar. Again, be nonjudgmental, but interrupt and politely ask for clarification if you hear any of the following:
   - Abstract, high-level, theoretical, or vague

language (*You mentioned Concept X. What does that refer to, specifically, for this particular case?*)

- Jargon, insider-speak, or acronyms (*I didn't understand that term. Is there a more common version?*)
- New words spilling out when you ask them why that changed variable made them feel more or less excited than before. DO NOT LET THESE PASS BY UNREMARKED. Call them out. This is the moment when people feel some pressure to justify their choices, and when revelations might occur without their realizing it. This is also where an attentive listener is a researcher's best friend. You're the Sounding Board now. Play what they said back to them, and prompt them to greater precision. (*You just said a word that isn't in your research question. Is that a key variable in your study? If so, how would you rephrase your research question?*)

7. When you feel like the interviewee's responses to the variable changing are getting you both closer to the problem, shift gears. Share with them what you noticed and ask them to speculate about the problem that might explain the pattern in their excitement. (*Here are your responses to these variable changes. You said that these variables could be changed, meaning that you'd be interested in those cases too, and these other variables couldn't, meaning that they are somehow central to your agenda. If you had to guess, what would you say is the underlying problem that you are concerned with in this research project?*)

8. Hopefully your conversation will be an insightful and enjoyable one. In any event, be sure to thank your interviewee for their time!

- Making all the same mistakes listed under the COV exercise in chapter 4, including changing variables too slightly to make a difference to the fundamentals of the research project
- Not explaining the goals and procedure of COV in advance of the interview
- Being too shy or deferential to ask follow-up questions or clarification questions
- Not writing things down

After your interview session, take stock. How do you feel? How did COV go for both of you? Was it easier or harder than you expected? Did you notice when your interviewee slipped in a new variable? Did you find yourself staying nonjudgmental? Would you want to do this again, with them or with someone else?

You certainly will have gotten to know your interviewee better. Maybe you've even helped them to get to know themself better. Your gentle probing, and challenging and naive but persistent questioning, may well have helped them to become more self-centered researchers. You hopefully will also have made the pleasant discovery that one of the best ways to be a student is to be a teacher or mentor. This is getting over yourself in the best way—by making a habit of helping other researchers become more centered on their Problem.

Through the exercises you have just completed, you have accomplished a major mental leap. You have separated the field-specific *case*—with all its specificity and field jargon—from the generalized *problem*, which cuts across the grain of one field and extends into other fields. This mental change liberates you from the narrow view of a field as mere Topic

Land, which mistakenly believes that studies are relevant to one another only if they share a topic. You now have techniques to determine what really matters to different researchers in your field and how to diagnose the problem within a study that might or might not articulate it clearly. (Of course, you might encounter studies that lack a problem and remain stuck in Topic Land, but you can make these useful to you too.) You have gained a better appreciation for the problem that motivates the research of your Sounding Board or another researcher you trust. And for your own research explorations, you now know why you need not—and should not—just stay "on topic."

Beyond your current project, you have gained a more fluid approach to navigating a field, one that is sensitive to the concerns of other Problem Collectives within it. You have acquired multiple techniques for figuring out which parts of it are most useful to you, while remaining centered.

You'll never be done with this process once and for all because your Field is not static. It keeps adding and shedding members. New publications keep appearing. And, if you look, you will continue to uncover earlier studies that you didn't know existed.

Now, having sorted out your Field by Problem Collective, you need to figure out how to talk to the members of your Field.

TRY THIS NOW: Rewrite for Your Field
The goal: *Informed by your Problem Collective, to learn to write about your Problem in a way that your Field will understand, and to see your Problem with "Field eyes."*

In chapter 4, you wrote for your Collective. Writing for your Collective required you to eliminate all of the insider language (or jargon) and secret codes that might be easily understandable to those in your Field, but which needed to be rephrased in order to be meaningful to members of your Collective.

Now it's time to switch audiences and repeat the process, but with a couple of new goals. Your Field, as mentioned above, is populated mostly by people who are not part of your Problem Collective and are uninterested in your Problem. Why write for them? Put another way, what might be the value of looking at your Problem with Field eyes?

When you have to explain your project to someone who doesn't care about your Problem (or thinks they don't), several good things might happen. You might, of course, change their minds about the relevance of your Problem. People are not static; they can be persuaded by arguments and evidence, and you might create a new ally. You might help Collective members within your Field find one another through your work. Even if they don't become members of your Collective, you may deepen their questions for other explorations. In any case, you will change your Field.

Our goal is to make sure that what you've written is comprehensible. Look over the first draft of your proposal description and highlight any terms that people in your Field are unlikely to know or be familiar with. These might include the following:

- Concepts and theories
- Key authors relevant to the "Problem Collective" dimensions of your research
- Key debates or arguments among members of your Collective
- Personal names
- Names of institutions or organizations

- Titles
- Acronyms
- Periodizations
- Topics

Highlight your enthusiasms (and other scholars'), just as you did your insider language when writing for your Collective.

Other benefits to rewriting for your Field are personal. In chapter 1, we mentioned that boredom can be a wonderful teacher in the early phases of a project, and gave examples of the ways it can help you to articulate and conceptualize your concerns. We also spoke about the importance of facing up to your own boredoms without judgment. If, upon telling someone about your concern with X, you are terribly bored by every association—A, B, C, and D—they make with X, you should not judge yourself. Don't force yourself to be interested in anything, even if it's Important (with a capital *I*).

Boredom is back, but this time to help you in a different way. When you rewrite for your Field, as opposed to your Collective, you will, alas, need to venture into what you consider to be the less compelling features or logical associations with your core questions and problems. These will not be encounters with boredom that help you grasp more clearly who you are as a thinker, and what your Problem truly is—they will simply be topics and questions that you are already fully aware of, but just find painfully dull.

This is an essential process, for a number of reasons. Here are two:

1. **Engaged readers make better researchers.** By engaging seriously and in good faith with such areas and questions, you are engaging seriously and respectfully with your Field mates *as members*

of Problem Collectives other than your own. You have to contend with other agendas. They don't find these aspects of your work "boring"—for them, this is likely the reason they picked up your work, came to hear you speak, or are bothering to engage with you at all. They find these problems disturbing, fascinating, and worthy of long-term (even career-long) engagement. To dismiss these aspects of your work as uninteresting or unworthy of contemplation, as you can imagine, is no small insult. For some, it would be the same thing as dismissing as insignificant a problem that keeps them up at night, and for some, their whole reason for becoming a researcher in the first place. It is deeply personal. By contrast, a good-faith engagement with these questions is your way of acknowledging and taking seriously that your Field mates may belong to Problem Collectives entirely different from your own.

2. **Engagement can lead you to discover and embrace new research problems.** Engagement of the kind we are encouraging here benefits your own intellectual and personal growth. Sometimes—although by no means always—the labor of seriously engaging with "boring" issues can subtly transform you and change your own perspective. Sometimes, you even begin to catch glimpses of these problems, seeing them as if through the eyes of those collectives who consider these problems fundamental to their identity. Even better, you find your own way of "translating" these problems into your own language, stumbling upon a wording or a phrasing that, in a flash of insight, suddenly

finds *you* disturbed. You realize that, all this time, it wasn't the problem itself that was "boring" to you; it's simply that you had never heard the problem phrased in a way that made sense to you. But now that you have, suddenly you find yourself kept awake at night.

And remember: it is perfectly good and natural if your first draft—even your fifth or sixth—is still inward-looking. The point is that every subsequent edit and draft should move steadily outward, opening up, equipping uninitiated readers, and inviting them into your Problem. Make your Problem their Problem. Disturb them by showing them—in terms *they* will understand—what disturbs you. Your work needs to make arguments, to be sure, but just as much it needs to equip a reader with everything they need to know in order to understand your argument.

SOUNDING BOARD:
Find a Sounding Board in Your Field

A Sounding Board in your Field will bring another perspective to your evolving research project. Consider reaching out to someone who is not at your institution—someone who is not your boss or who has no personally vested interest in the outcome of your study, besides their professional goodwill. They can help you to ensure that your manner of expressing ideas will be comprehensible to your peers. They will help you to identify sources you might have overlooked. They will help you anticipate which questions about your primary source (your cereal box, so to speak) have been asked and answered by others in your Field. Again, show them your research proposal and solicit their response, whether written or oral. And (you guessed it) make sure to say *Thank you*.

Welcome to Your Field

Membership in a Field can be rewarding. You'll find that in a field, as in a Problem Collective, groups of researchers develop a certain *esprit de corps*. Curiosity, relentlessness, and generosity are the ingredients fueling their productivity and inspiration. One of the benefits of a field is the productive friction between the different Problem Collectives therein. Their disturbance becomes your disturbance, and suddenly your own research achieves a new dimensionality for you. You suddenly see a part of your field in 3D.

You are still a problem. Always keep in mind that the scale, ambition, and brilliance of your question is never limited to the scale of the specific project you end up working on. In fact, just the opposite: the more brilliant and resonant your question, the more it will spill out from the confines of your project, often in ways you haven't anticipated.

6. How to Begin

. . . .

You're nearing the end of this book. Are you feeling a little bit relieved? Ceaseless self-examination of the sort you've been doing is no one's idea of a vacation. It's hard work, and it's almost over.

Take a moment to consider the work you've done thus far. You are in conscious possession of a problem, and you've transformed it into the beginnings of a project. You can find sources and generate questions like nobody's business. You know how to stay centered in your Problem as you engage with various research communities. You've found your Collective. You've navigated and engaged your Field. You've written and rewritten about your Problem for both of them.

What's left to do?

To write.

More specifically, to write *from the self-center you have created*. Not from a narrow sense of self, but rather the expansive self that you have been developing and discovering through the course of this book.

Now that you've found your center, it's time to rewrite with centeredness.

Remember: your center is not some kind of military base or fortification designed to repel outsiders and protect insiders. Nor is it a location on a map. Your center is, as a researcher, a center of gravity that keeps you squarely over your own two feet at all times, even as you continue to move forward and change. To be centered is to be comfortable in your own skin.

It is a self-possession you carry with you on your research journey. From time to time, you may get lost on your journey or feel knocked off-balance or momentarily lose your sense of self. But having found the problem at the center of your research, you'll be able to return to it, time and again.

Finding your center is empowering. Being a self-centered researcher is not just about having interests or being interesting. It's about being confident enough to discriminate between the choices you will face throughout the research process, and to make wise decisions about how to spend your time. To know, in your bones, what is really worth doing. Whether you have just one project to finish this month, or a career's worth of research in your future, you'll have to choose between an array of promising ideas and exciting possibilities. Some of these might speak to your core problem, but most won't. Others may praise you for coming up with this or that neat idea, but as a self-centered researcher you will be able to respond to such encouragement by asking yourself: *Yes, this is interesting — but is this part of my Problem?* When you are centered, you are able to say "No, thank you" to scintillating ideas and flashy, passing thoughts, things that your uncentered alter ego would jump at without knowing why. The uncentered researcher feels tempted to chase every good idea that comes along; the centered researcher is discerning.

So, to return to our point above, now that you've done all of this wonderful work on finding your center, your last exercise in this book is to write *from* it.

Don't Worry. It's All Writing.

This final instruction — that now is the time "to write" — might seem like a profound buzzkill. Your fleeting sense of relief gives way to anxiety, even dread. Writing, as we all know, is the "hard part." What is more, it's not as if the exercises in this book have marched you step-by-step through the expected parts of a traditional thesis. You don't even have an introduction, much less a conclusion. You have hardly any polished prose. You have no footnotes. You don't have anything! *I've done a whole book's worth of exercises and I still have all my writing to do?!*

Well, guess what? *You've been writing this entire time.*

Let's take stock of just how much writing you've produced so far. Assuming you've given yourself time to complete all or most of the exercises, this means that, at this very moment, your notebook or hard drive contains the following:

- A list of search results on your topic that jumped out at you, along with your ruminations about why they did
- A list of search results on the same topic that bored you, along with your thoughts about why they did
- A list of "small" factual questions about a single primary source
- A list of assumptions that make each of these small questions possible (i.e., the "premises" of these questions)
- A list of search results of primary sources, based on a refined search query (using terms from your "small" questions)
- The results of the Cereal Box Challenge, namely a worksheet containing multiple genres of questions about your chosen primary source and plenty of ideas about the next primary sources you might look for
- A bibliography or a list of secondary sources, from both your Problem Collective and your Field
- An extended brainstorm about your envisioned ideal primary sources, how you might use them, and where they might be found
- A decision matrix to help you craft a project that fits your personhood, as well various determinative factors

- A first draft of a research proposal, full of names, acronyms, jargon, and other types of language comprehensible only to members of your Field
- A printout of the research proposal that you have highlighted to identify all instances of insider language
- A revised version of the research proposal in lay language comprehensible to your Problem Collective
- Your worksheets from the "Change One Variable" exercise, including an improved research question, and lists of the fungible vs. non-negotiable elements of that question
- Your worksheets from the "Before and After" exercise, with ideas about how the case you're working on might fit into a bigger story about your Problem
- Notes from your "Change One Variable" interview of a Sounding Board
- Advice from your Sounding Boards from various stages of your project-conceptualization work

What is more, chances are high that, while reading through the primary and secondary sources that spoke to you, you may also have done one or more of the following—*all of which are also forms of writing*:

- Brainstorming
- Outlining
- Emailing
- Underlining, highlighting, and making marginal notes in a book or an article
- Scribbling on napkins, take-out menus, subway schedules
- Text messages
- Social media posts
- Blog entries
- To-do lists
- Audio recordings

All of this is writing. *All of it.*

You've also already begun the process of refining and consolidating your ideas in writing. You wrote a research proposal based solely on the introspection you did in part 1. You rewrote your proposal for your Problem Collective with the aim of reaching a wider community centered on a common problem. You also rewrote for your Field, navigating its various Problem Collectives to explain how your project might have implications for others. In short, you've rewritten your project several times while supposedly still on the starting block.

Wait a minute, you say.

This isn't real writing! At best, this is "note-taking" or "journaling" or "prewriting." Most of what I have are fragmentary notes, and countless questions. Maybe I do have a few transcribed quotes, a few new facts and sources, and a rough proposal, but I certainly haven't begun writing the study itself.

You've done more than just "begin." You've prepared yourself for the next phase of research, which—like the next one, and the one after that—requires that you begin yet again.

So start!

Take those fragmentary notes, and transform them into complete sentences and paragraphs.

Place those quotes in your working document, and write down why they matter to your research problem.

Look at the many self-reflections you have produced thus far and identify passages from your notes that you feel capture the underlying "problem" of your work in compelling language. Add them to your proposal or working document.

Take the bibliographic references you've copied and pasted—those that jumped out at you so long ago—and expand them into fully formed footnotes and bibliographic entries.

Steps like these are part of the creative research process. These are the materials out of which research papers, articles, and books are made. A film is, put crudely, footage shot and edited. A painting is a series of chromatic brush-strokes on a surface. A book is a collection of words, sentences, paragraphs, notes, and figures. To be sure, you can continually work at making your collection of words more clear, compelling, empirical, rigorous, or elegant. Just keep in mind that, if your goal is "to write," any and every act of putting pen to paper or fingers to keys is part of that process.

Writing is not a pristine, reverent act. It's a messy, scrappy affair.

And so we invite you to look over what you've produced thus far, and appreciate that you've been writing this entire time. While you probably have not been writing in clear, po-etic passages all this time, the writing you have produced is a valuable type of raw material. As you sift through all your writings, you will choose what to abandon and what to preserve. You will refine most of what you save, and re-word nearly all of it. You will move from all those fragmen-tary writings you have now to paragraphs of polished, well-structured prose.

So, when we say that now is the time "to write," what we really mean is that now is the time to bring all of the writing you have already done together into one place, and to begin that process of sifting, selecting, structuring, and clarifying.

TRY THIS NOW: Create "Draft 0"

The goal: *To consolidate all of the different types of writing you have produced during the Self-Centered Research pro-cess thus far into a single document.*

Create a "Draft 0." Not a "first draft" or "Draft 1" that re-quires lots of new writing. All you need to do for the mo-ment is to bring together all of your writing thus far into a single digital file.

Here is your checklist of items to compile:

Digital notes. If you've been using your computer, phone, or tablet to take notes, you might have them saved in a variety of files, formats, and locations. Now is the time to copy and paste all of these into your unified Draft 0. This includes the draft research proposal you wrote in chapter 3, as well as those you rewrote for your Collective and your Field. Don't worry about where to paste each item. Dump them anywhere. Structure does not matter at this point.

Handwritten notes. If you've taken notes on loose-leaf paper, in bound journals, or on napkins, transcribe them all *word for word* into Draft 0. Resist the temptation to rewrite just yet.

Underlinings, highlights, and marginalia. Return to any primary or secondary source that you have marked up in one form or another. Transcribe these notes into your digital file. Be sure also to transcribe full bibliographic information as well, to identify the primary or secondary source you marked up.

As you pull these items together in Draft 0, also do the following:

Tidy up (but only if it doesn't bog you down). While transcribing fragmentary notes or thoughts, you might find yourself correcting misspellings in your original digital notes, or expanding fragmentary notes into complete sentences. If you can do this without bogging down the progress of consolidation, go for it. *But you don't have to.* There will be plenty of time to do this later on. If you do find yourself getting slowed down with efforts to reword, copyedit, expand, develop, and perfect, remind yourself that Draft 0 is meant to be a mindless, mechanical act of consolidation. That's all. Just get your stuff in one place, in one format.

Note down "self-evidence." One important exception to the Do Not Revise Yet rule: during this transcription and consolidation process, stay centered and "in tune" with yourself. You are still hooked up to that EKG machine. Continue to use introspective techniques as you revisit your earlier writings. Pay attention to any new thoughts or questions that surface while your consolidating your existing notes, and write those thoughts down *directly* into the Draft 0 digital file. This cannot bog you down; it is *always* time well spent.

By the end of this process, you will have a single file containing many thousands of words. It will be sloppy, un-grammatical, disjointed, and unstructured. It will be full of gaps and unfounded speculations.

Let it be all of these things.

This is not a final product. In fact, you should go out of your way to be messy and incoherent, because this will help you overcome, in one fell swoop, two of the most powerful inhibitors of the writing process:

1. The fear of judgment
2. The fear of the blank page

By consolidating the messiest Draft 0 possible, you over-come any fear of embarrassment—the fear of writing something incoherent, incorrect, or immature. You over-come it, strangely enough, by creating the most embar-rassingly incoherent document you can imagine. Then you discover that the world didn't end.

Likewise, there's simply no time to be afraid of the blank page. You give it no chance to exist. That pristine page that dares you to produce a thought worthy of it disappears, as your copying and pasting fills the blank page—and then another and another page—with text. Incoherent text, perhaps, but text nonetheless. Draft 0 helps you to overcome your page fright. "What would I do if I *weren't afraid*?" Draft 0 answers that question for you. It won't cure you of all your writerly fears and hang-ups, but it won't give the first big fear you face any time to intervene. As messy as Draft 0 will be, it will also contain the following:

- Critical evidence
- The makings of a robust base of primary and secondary sources
- Quotations that you found in primary and secondary sources
- Key figures
- Questions that are essential to your purpose

As chaotic as it looks, it may also contains moments of brilliance—perhaps more than a few.

See What You Mean: Writing Draft 1

Having produced a consolidated file with all of your writings, the key now is to begin the process of moving from Draft 0 to Draft 1: a process of sorting, grouping, copyediting, sectioning, titling, and other forms of editing. Throughout this process, remember this bit of time-tested wisdom: *the best essays and books aren't written, they're rewritten.*

Sometimes, writing is the manifestation of a preexisting thought—a coherent, ready-to-express idea. Most of the time, it's not. Writing is, in its most fundamental sense, an act of *estrangement*, of *alienation*, of *discovery*. It is a process of literally externalizing your thoughts. You turn what was in your brain and in your body into something unfamiliar and new, so that you can see it with fresh eyes and then improve it. To "get it out on the page" means to take something that is within you, and put it in front of you, so that your mind has a fighting chance to think critically about it. You cannot see your own eyes — they are the things that see. You need to put it out in front of you. You can't think your own mind — it is the thing that thinks. You need to put it in front of you, estrange it, look at it. Then you can re-internalize it, then alienate it again, and again, and again. This sounds philosophical, but it's really the key to creating Draft 2, Draft 3, and Draft 4.

This is how writing *really works*.

This is what writing *really does*.

As a self-centered researcher, you are prepared to become your own writing partner. You can offer yourself the same kind of clear advice that is usually so much easier to give to *other* researchers. Just as you can readily see the argument that lies beneath the surface of your colleague's or classmate's or friend's opaque wording, you can do that very same thing for yourself, one draft at a time.

This is not an easy or natural thing to do. It takes work. Repeated and rigorous introspection. By now you are familiar with your subject matter. Critically, you are also familiar with the way you *think* about your subject matter. Now the challenge is to see if there are any gaps or inconsistencies between the two, and, if there are, to decide what to do.

The key to making such decisions is, as always, to *notice what you are noticing about yourself as you review, revise, and expand your project.*

Start by reading your Draft 0 out loud, word for word. As you do, utilize the techniques of self-reflection that you've been developing over the course of this book. *Pay attention to yourself as you read your own work.* Are you getting bored? Lost? Make a note of that. Are you laughing with delight at a certain turn of phrase? Notice that too. As you read this sentence or that paragraph, are you getting a sense of what you should write next, or what sources you should look for? Write a note at that point in your draft. Do you feel a sense of satisfaction when the author (i.e., you) gets to the point that the evidence supports? Or are you feeling dissatisfied or even annoyed over how long you've been taking to get to the point (even if you get there eventually)? Does the flow of a certain section pivot or segue to a new thought too often, or is there a nice pacing to the argumentation?

Be realistic in your reading. Do the kinds of things that regular readers do when they read a thesis, an article, or a book chapter: take breaks. Stop midway, go read an email, pour yourself a cup of tea or coffee, come back and pick up where you left off. Are you able to find your way back in? Is the flow of ideas clear? How about the language? In short, try to experience your own writing exactly the way a third-party reader would, and then see how your work holds up as a reading experience.

TRY THIS NOW: Move from 0 to 1

The goal: *To create a "Draft 1"—a document with a (very) preliminary sense of structure—by making an initial pass at sorting, grouping, and editing your consolidated writings from Draft 0.*

Here are just some of the steps you can take to accomplish this transformation:

1. **Combine things that obviously go together.** Let's say you've already transcribed three quotes by the same person; but because you did so at different times, these quotes are scattered in different locations in your Draft 0. Cut and paste them into the same place in the document. Likewise, maybe your notes on a particular figure, event, or idea are scattered here and there across your notes

in Draft 0. Bring those together as well. You may discover a good reason to redivide them later on—perhaps you want those three quotes in different parts of your final product—but for the meantime a good rule of thumb is to combine like things.

2. **Move all bibliographic entries to the end of the document.** This is one of the simplest parts of "combining similar things" and involves locating, cutting, and repasting any bibliographic citations you have in your notes at the end of the document (where they will eventually live, in the References, Works Cited, or Bibliography section of your work). Having them all in one place also makes it easier when the time comes to add all necessary in-text citations, footnotes, and/or endnotes.

3. **Experiment with combining things that *might* go together.** Let's say you perceive a possible connection between different parts of your notes, but one that is not obvious or straightforward. Maybe three fragmentary notes seem to orbit around a common theme that you might want to use as a key structural device in your Problem. These might become the focus of a section of your article, or a chapter of your thesis. Cut and paste those things into the same part of the document, and see what happens. Does the grouping feel coherent and compelling? If so, try developing it. Does the connection feel forced? Then maybe try a different thematic grouping, or simply leave it alone for now and come back later when you have more clarity, or have consulted more primary and secondary sources.

4. **Pay attention to "self-evidence" as you rearrange**

chunks of your document. As you explore potential ways to group your notes, what you'll soon find is that your draft is taking on something of a preliminary structure. Things are no longer completely scattered or random. They are starting to take shape. As you get deeper into this process, don't lose sight of self-evidence. Listen for any new thoughts, questions, phrasings, or ideas that crop up while you do this, and make sure to write these ideas into Draft 1. Think about *where* makes the most sense. You could place them near a given thematic cluster that inspired the thoughts; but if you find them hard to place, just put them all in one place at the beginning or the end of Draft 1. Treat that place like a catchall "miscellaneous folder" and worry about how to process those thoughts later.

5. **Where possible, put those chunks into a rough sequence.** If parts of your document seem out of order, reorder them. Let's say that you've just combined three quotes by the same person, all of which are from the 1920s. Then you notice that what directly precedes it in the document is another set of quotations from the 1960s. Just switch the order. You can reorder things later on if necessary, but at this stage, it's a good rule of thumb to keep things chronological. Likewise, if you discover that three of your chunks all deal with a shared theme, try grouping those chunks into their own section—just to see what happens. It might not be obvious what "order" or "sequence" to put them in, and that's fine for now. But don't force it: if one or more chunks don't offer up any

obvious answer for where they "belong," just leave them be.

6. **Add titles to sections of the document.** Remember how we suggested that you give your movie a title before you've shot a single frame? Well, this kind of envisioning is a *continual* part of the research process, and it applies not only to the title of your work in progress, but also to the sections inside of it. So, once you've gotten far enough along in the process of grouping your fragments of text, and then combining those groups into sections, take the next step of naming those sections. Doing so will help you not only to work with your draft more efficiently, but also to structure your thoughts.

7. **Develop your writerly voice.** Are your verbs precise or generic? Is your vocabulary varied or repetitive? Are your claims clear or evasive? Do you notice yourself relying on a narrow set of phrases, clichés, and devices for transitioning between ideas? Draft 1 is a good time to begin thinking about your voice as a writer. Become aware of the way that figurative language commits us to arguments that we might be unaware of. Historians, for example, often resort (sometimes excessively) to biological metaphors like "growth," "seminal moments," "evolution," "stems," and so forth. Novice researchers often pick up such terms quickly in their effort to emulate authorities in their chosen field, but established members sometimes use such terms uncritically too. The important thing to realize is that these terms are not "neutral." They shape thought in profound (if subliminal) ways, and thus the course and outcomes of research.

Check to see if you have been using such language conventions uncritically, and rephrase if you have.

8. **Keep killing your acronyms.** You've now done a couple passes at rewriting for your Collective and your Field, but the process of improving the precision and clarity of your language is far from over. We all miss some jargon during the first cull. More importantly, every time we produce new prose, we easily lapse into using words that obscure rather than clarify our subject matter and purpose. Be vigilant about insider language throughout the rewriting process.

9. **Add footnotes, endnotes, or other necessary citations.** Start the process of tracking your sources of information systematically. If you plan on using any of the direct quotes you transcribed, add the footnote now, and include a full reference. Choose a single formatting style for references that you will use throughout the project, and make sure to apply it uniformly. There is *nothing* more draining than getting to the end of a long research journey and having to spend hours or days cleaning up messy notes.

Perfection Is Boring

We sometimes celebrate "perfection" in books, music, images, works of art. The truth is, if those things were perfect, they would be painfully boring. A "perfect" thing does not need us. Even a powerful microscope would reveal no flaw or foothold on its smooth surface. It would leave us no "way in," nothing to say. There would be no need for anything to exist beyond its own precious self.

The same is true of research and writing. If your work is "perfect" from the moment of completion, you leave us nothing to say. There is nothing to be added or subtracted, struggled with or contemplated. It does not engage. Your work would be waterproof, criticism-proof, improvement-proof, *thought-proof.* Is that really what you want?

If you have ever been fortunate enough to encounter a work of art, scholarship, or creation that strikes you as perfect, you have probably come to this realization: "perfect" things are perfected not by the author, but by *us* as readers, viewers, and listeners.

The goal of research, then, is not to produce a precious artifact for others to admire. It is to create a continual, ever-renewing process of betterment — of improving and *perfecting* things.

Research projects sometimes come to us well built, other times full of holes. Consider the sponge. Before it comes into contact with anything, it is shot through with holes; and yet after coming into contact with the world, it has those gaps suffused and filled with material supplied by something other than itself.

A research project cannot be perfect. But a research project can be built and executed in such a way that, in addition to posing and answering a limited number of specific questions, can take the shape of an intellectual sponge, leaving ample space within its structure for its *audience* to fill it up with their own material: their questions, their Problems, their cases. Leave it to others to perfect your research. Leave them a way in.

As you'll have gathered by now, the goal of the Self-Centered Research process, of all that introspection, is to create the conditions for such perfection to occur. That's why — as we said at the beginning — you are the one who will complete the composition of this book. You are the one who will perfect it.

SOUNDING BOARD: Talk to Yourself

You are now self-centered enough—and you know we mean this in a good way—to be your own Sounding Board. Throughout this book, you've received a lot of advice from us. Hopefully, you have also sought out and received advice from one or more external Sounding Boards. Now is the time to assess which parts of the Self-Centered Research process have been useful for you.

This does not mean that you now reject external advice. On the contrary, by now you should be in regular contact with your Problem Collective and more closely enmeshed in your Field.

Take out your notes. Glance over the table of contents of this book again. Look at your notes and the contents side by side, and think about which parts of the Self-Centered Research process have been most useful to you, and which parts might be useful in the future.

Consider these questions:

- Which exercises do I want to repeat?
- Which exercises might I want to modify in some way, to suit my own purposes?
- Which exercises do I think I can improve on?
- Which bored me, and why?
- Which do I want to share with others? Whom could these exercises help?
- Which ways of thinking about my relation to members of my Field, or people who share my Problem, have been most useful to me?
- Which notes do I want to expand on or revise first?

Welcome to Self-Centered Research

By putting yourself through the Self-Centered Research process you have changed who you are. You are not just the same person with "more skills and more stuff." Yes, you have new skills. Yes, you have a portfolio of all the things you have written thus far. Yes, you have the beginnings of a research project. But, equally importantly, you have now forged a new *disposition* as a self-centered researcher. This mindset frees you from the common misperceptions and phobias and inhibitions and insecurities that hobble so many members of the research community — or that dissuade people from becoming researchers in the first place. You are a centered and mobile unit that can interact with fellow researchers of various fields with confidence, insight, and equanimity. You are not intimidated by other researchers' accomplishments, nor by the knowledge that self-improvement is an ongoing process.

Welcome to a wonderful way of life.

What's Next in Your Research Journey?

. . . .

While reading this book, you will have gained new ideas about what research is and how to undertake it. We hope that we have also persuaded you to make research a habit — a regular part of your life. You should now be launched on your new research project. But we hope that you will look beyond your current project and envision ways to apply the principles and strategies you've learned in this book to other problems.

What lies ahead for you? To take another course in your Field? To become a professional researcher? You have a wide array of possibilities and opportunities for the pursuit of research.

Notice that we did not say *academic* research, necessarily. Research of any kind. The researcher's life is a rich, rewarding, and critical one — it's one that doesn't stand by and complacently consume commonsense truths passed down to us. The research disposition is not merely skeptical. Reflexive skepticism, after all, is no more reliable than reflexive credulity. A researcher is skeptical *and* committed to undertaking the challenging work of turning skepticism into specific questions, and then to seeking out answers. The researcher is equipped to stress-test and evaluate the claims made by others, not necessarily because they have memorized all of the facts, but because they know how such claims are built in the first place — and deeper still, they know how research questions are built and refined.

Find a New Problem and Start a New Project

The goal: *To begin planning your research future by thinking about what other problems matter to you, and envisioning how you might turn them into research projects.*

When you find your center, you gain a superpower: the ability to discern when your Problem itself is changing, or perhaps when new problems are starting to take shape in your mind. Thus far, all of our examples and exercises have operated under the assumption of "one person, one problem." For the sake of simplicity, we've pretended that every scholar has one problem that motivates and generates their work. Likewise, we've treated problems as something like a mathematical constant: an independent variable that stays exactly the same across time.

While some of this is true—problems can and do endure for years, sometimes decades—this does not mean that problems never change, or that a single scholar might not be grappling with several problems. (To repeat our earlier advice, however, if you tallied up your "problems" and discovered dozens, then you're probably dealing with "interests" or "curiosities," and not "problems" in the sense we use this word in the book. In that case, you might benefit from reviewing chapter 2.)

Problems change because people change. As you move through life, your Problem will transform. It may dissolve entirely. It may linger, and yet lose some of its power over you. For reasons we cannot always explain, sometimes problems that once cast a spell over us can, with the passage of time, feel small in retrospect. And a new problem, or problems, can take shape: new and enduring disturbances that keep you up at night, and hound you day after day, for years on end. To reiterate: we are talking about problems as productive and motivating research concerns.

We are talking about disturbances that are personal but can nevertheless be analyzed and evaluated with a critical, independent eye.

Like the movement of tectonic plates under the ocean surface, the disappearance of one's long-standing intellectual problem, and the formation of a new one, can be hard to detect. But, as a self-centered researcher, you will be better equipped than most to discern such subtle shifts. You are now attuned to take note of changes that your prior self would likely have missed.

So, with all of this in mind, one thing you might do right now is to identify a second problem and start a *new* project.

This might seem like peculiar advice, especially since your first research project is only just starting. But it's not too early to begin building a small repertoire of projects. Yes, you'll continue working on your current project. But what will you do when you need a break from Project 1? Or when Project 1 is complete? Start planning ahead now.

As we noted in the introduction, research is not a linear process. By that, we mean also that it's possible—even desirable—to have multiple ideas and projects in play at a time. Is Project 1 exhausting you, or somehow not motivating you this week? Perhaps you can shift your attention to Project 2. You'll be making progress on solving another problem you care about, but it will feel like a respite.

Then again, a single problem can (and often does) manifest itself in more than one project. You may well discover that Project 2 is connected to your core problem—maybe explicitly, or perhaps at a slight remove. Working on a couple of projects (not too many!) can let you view your Problem from different vantage points, like a battery of cameras mounted in different places but all trained on the same subject.

Finally, remember: the exercises in this book are repeatable, and can be used to launch any new project, from your first to your fifteenth. We use them ourselves. No matter if you're an undergraduate student or an emeritus professor, a rookie journalist or a Pulitzer Prize winner, the beginning of the research process is always dynamic, often confusing, and always full of possibility. Harness that potential.

COMMONLY MADE MISTAKES

- Thinking that research is a linear process, or that you have to finish Project 1 before you start Project 2
- Mistaking many areas of interest as each being a separate problem
- Trying to take on too many projects at one time

TRY THIS NOW: Help Someone Else

The goal: *To use the Self-Centered Research philosophy, techniques, skills, and exercises to help other researchers find their center.*

Getting over yourself, like becoming a self-centered researcher, is not just something you think about, but rather something you *do* . . . over and over again.

As you become ever more familiar with the process of Self-Centered Research—of crafting and refining questions, rather than trying to answer them prematurely—you hone your abilities to analyze, appreciate, and advance not only your own scholarship, but also the research practices of others.

Imagine a world of centered researchers. No, don't just imagine it—help make it a reality.

You're ready. You've gained multiple techniques for

centering your research. You appreciate at first hand the value of a varied toolkit for research decision-making. If you don't feel you've mastered a certain technique yet, repeat the exercise. You have the capacity to offer feedback attuned to the needs of others: work by friends, colleagues, students, and even mentors.

Don't assume that any of them have gone through what you just have. Even if they are competent, accomplished, distinguished, even eminent researchers, don't assume that they have already found their center. We are all working on finding our centers. Even if a fellow researcher *has* found their center, remember: centers shift over the course of a career, and a lifetime, and we all have to recenter ourselves at certain points in our lives.

So all you need to do to make a difference in another researcher's life is to apply the processes outlined in this book. When you read their work, or listen to their explanations, ask yourself:

- Are they falling victim to that common mistake of "trying to sound smart"?
- Are they concealing their motivating problems behind insider jargon, feats of eloquence, or invocation of "gaps in the literature"?
- Are they able to articulate their research concerns in ways that successfully disturb you as a third-party listener—as someone who might not care at all about their *case* but is certainly receptive to their *Problem*?
- Are they aware of who and where their Problem Collective is?
- Are they burying the most important and most critical insights in random places in the middle of their study?

When reading their research proposals, abstracts, or outlines, do you feel well guided, or do you get lost in the data and terminology? Do you feel invited into the problem, or do you find yourself tripping over insider-speak, unidentified persons and events, and unexplained acronyms?

As your ability to analyze your own research deepens, helping someone else will feel effortless by comparison.

In short, you are ready to become someone else's Sounding Board. We think you should.

If you're not sure how to help others in this way, here are several ready-made ways to get involved:

- **Writing partnerships/workshops**, in which the members offer good-faith critiques of one another's works in progress. Organize your own!
- **Manuscript reviews**, which are confidential reviews of unpublished scholarly studies, written for a dual audience: the editors of the journal or publishing house who will decide whether or not to publish a particular work, and the author. Their goals are to offer constructive criticism of the work in progress, and a judgment about whether or not it meets the quality standards for publication.
- **Book reviews**, which are public appraisals of a published work of scholarship, credited to a named reviewer. These pieces of writing offer an opinion on the specific merits and shortcomings of a single study, and explain its contributions to a field of inquiry.
- **State-of-the-field essays**, which identify current trends in the field and summarize and appraise the contributions of several works of scholarship toward answering its questions and solving its problems. These are synthetic reviews on high-

level conceptual or philosophical issues, for which evaluation of specific studies is a secondary priority.
- **Conference and workshop presentations**, which, depending on field, can be of studies in progress or completed studies. Typically, the researcher summarizes their findings, followed by a critique by a discussant (or panel) and comments or questions from the audience.
- For more ideas, visit whereresearchbegins.com.

You can contribute to the advancement of research by participating in any of these activities. Help someone in your Field. Help someone in your Collective.

Be *our* Sounding Board.

Reach out. You can help us by sharing your experience and ideas. How is the Self-Centered Research process working for you? Have you had success in adapting or modifying any exercises? We welcome your suggestions for improvement. Research, as we've said all along, is a collaborative and iterative process. This book represents just one small step in expanding a community.

We hope that you, like us, are in research for the long haul.

Acknowledgments

. . . .

This book has been eighteen years in the making.

During that time, we have amassed incalculable debts, and to express them fully would require more pages than you have just read. Simply put, we wish to thank our families, especially Chiara and Julie, our colleagues near and far, the amazing team at the University of Chicago Press, especially Karen, and (as coauthors and friends should) each other.

We dedicate this book to our students, not only at Stanford University and the University of British Columbia, but also at Columbia University, where the two of us met as students and stepped into the classroom for the first time as teachers.

And it doesn't end here. *Where Research Begins*, we hope, will mark a new beginning in how you — and we — think about, talk about, teach, and practice research.

We hope you will join us in this endeavor. In fact, by reading this book, you already have.

So, thank you.

Further Reading

. . . .

The following is a selective list of books and articles that have been useful to us in thinking about research philosophies and methods. You can find a longer list with annotated recommendations at whereresearchbegins.com.

Booth, Wayne C., Gregory G. Colomb, Joseph M. Williams, Joseph Bizup, and William T. FitzGerald. *The Craft of Research*. 4th ed. Chicago: University of Chicago Press, 2016.

Caro, Robert A. *Working: Researching, Interviewing, Writing*. New York: Knopf, 2019.

Eco, Umberto. *How to Write a Thesis*. Translated by Caterina Mongiat Farina and Geoff Farina. Foreword by Francesco Erspamer. Cambridge, MA: MIT Press, 2015.

Gerard, Philip. *The Art of Creative Research: A Field Guide for Writers*. Chicago: University of Chicago Press, 2017.

Graff, Gerald, and Cathy Birkenstein. *They Say/I Say: The Moves That Matter in Academic Writing*. New York: W.W. Norton, 2018.

Index